COOKING
WITH
BOOZE

GEORGE HARVEY BONE
FOREWORD BY LUCY BAKER

Skyhorse Publishing

Skyhorse Publishing books may be purchased in bulk at special
discounts for sales promotion, corporate gifts, fund-raising, or
educational purposes. Special editions can also be created to specifi-
cations. For details, contact the Special Sales Department, Skyhorse
Publishing, 307 West 36th Street, 11th Floor, New York, NY 10018
or info@skyhorsepublishing.com.

Visit our website at www.skyhorsepublishing.com.

10 9 8 7 6 5 4 3 2

Library of Congress Cataloging-in-Publication
Data is available on file.

Cover artwork courtesy of the author

ISBN: 978-1-5107-2336-8
eISBN: 978-1-5107-3184-4

Printed in the United States of America

CONTENTS

BEER

CIDER

VODKA

WHISKY

RUM

BRANDY

TEQUILA

OTHER SPIRITS & LIQUEURS

FOREWORD

George Harvey Bone and I are kindred spirits (pun intended). Ever since the idea for my own cookbook, *The Boozy Baker*, first popped into my head, I've been obsessed with infusing cakes, cookies, pies, puddings, and more with alcohol. Not only does it add a new dimension of luscious flavor, but it also makes them a whole lot more fun.

But, as George has taught me, that fun doesn't have to end with dessert. In *Cooking with Booze*, he demonstrates that wine, beer, and spirits can be incorporated into recipes for every meal of the day with incredibly delicious results. How about a bagel slathered with cream cheese and layered with homemade gravlax cured with fresh dill and brandy or Pernod? And I don't know about you, but I could certainly get used to topping my morning English muffin with Irish Whiskey Butter and Port Jelly . . . just as long as I can go back to bed afterwards.

When people think of boozy midday meals, the three-martini power lunch is what often comes to mind. Of course there's nothing wrong with that, but I've always been more of a soup and salad girl myself. A big bowl of Beer & Onion Soup with a side of Amaretto Spinach Salad is just the ticket (a slice of Bierbrood wouldn't hurt, either).

For cozy family dinners, there's Meatballs in Vodka Sauce, or Stout and Spicy Pasta with Chicken and Guinness, and for festive nights with friends you can't beat Roast Pork with Apple Stuffing and Cider Sauce or short ribs braised in not one, not two, but *three* entire bottles of red wine. Now that's sure to get the party started!

I'm no slouch when it comes to desserts, and the ones George includes here had me running to preheat my oven. Hello, Double Chocolate Grand Marnier Brownies! Where have you been all my life, Mojito Cupcakes? Baking with alcohol is devilish and decadent, and it has a hidden bonus, too. Not only does it infuse desserts with incredible flavor, that flavor actually improves over time. Trust me, day-old cake never tasted so good.

Throughout the pages of George's delightful little book, his humor and dry wit prove infectious. I confess to being one of those strange people who reads cookbooks like novels—I have a stack by my bed. Right now,

Cooking with Booze is at the top of the pile. Reading his droll descriptions of each recipe makes me want to meet up with George at the corner pub for a pint or two (on Whiskey and Honey Cake: "The sort of thing to sit down to after tossing a few cabers and killing a few Englishmen. With a nice cup of tea.")

While the recipes in George's book feel fresh and new, the tradition of cooking with alcohol spans the globe and goes back thousands of years to when it was first used as a way to preserve or cure food. So now that we have refrigerators and freezers, microwaves and *sous vide* machines, why do we still splash a little something into our dishes? Because it's fun, pure and simple. Adding a shot of rum or half a glass of wine is a terrific way to experiment with flavor, change things up, and breathe new life into an old recipe.

In addition, it's convenient. If you are like me and hate 1) letting opened bottles go to waste, and 2) recipes with a laundry list of ingredients, then *Cooking with Booze* is for you. George's recipes are a great way to use up whatever has been languishing in the back of your liquor cabinet or that bottle of wine you couldn't quite finish. And, since alcohol adds loads of complexity and flavor, you don't need a zillion other ingredients to cook up a quick and simple dinner that tastes restaurant-level delicious.

Finally, people have always turned to food—and to drink—for comfort when the going gets rough, and in times of celebration. (I for one would love to drown my sorrows in a pint of sweet Marsala Ice Cream, or raise a toast not with a flute of champagne, but with a broiled oyster swimming in champagne sauce.) It makes perfect sense to combine the two in one.

So forget the bar—it turns out the best place to drink is actually in your kitchen. It's time to pour yourself a glass and get cooking . . . with booze of course!

—Lucy Baker, author of *The Boozy Baker*

INTRODUCTION

It is not often that one feels the weight of history upon one's stomach, but this is such a time. The book you are holding in your hands contains some of the finest dishes known to man, bringing together as it does his two greatest pleasures: food, and booze.

These recipes have been gathered and archived by my family for many generations. The Bones are an ancient line, extending back through the famous de Beaune vintners of France who arrived with the Norman Conquest, and beyond, and in more recent times we have done our best to maintain the old ways.

My maternal grandfather was well known in the County for his extraordinary home-brews. He claimed to have invented a new kind of Pimms, and the release of his Attic Stout No 4 upon an unsuspecting village fête led directly to the defrocking of a bishop and the loss of an entire scout troop. My grandfather on my father's side was also a disciple of the finer things. After an unfortunate incident in the Sudan, when his regiment lost an entire Christmas' beer supply to a freak sandstorm, he swore never to go without again, and was heard to remark on his 90th birthday that he would consider putting more tonic than gin into his daily G&T, but the suggestion was unlikely to meet with much support.

The civilising effects of the gentler sex in the form of their respective wives went some way to persuading both of them to reduce their liquid intake and increase their solids, leading directly to many of the recipes set down upon these pages. I learnt much from these fine ladies – not least my grandmother's assertion that "the difference between a good cook and a great cook is half a pound of butter."

I urge you to heed such words as you peruse this compendium, and consider what you may learn from it. Be liberal in your measures, and adventurous in your sampling. If you don't have the stated ingredients to hand, substitute freely, and if you come across obscure terminology and foodstuffs that bewilder you, then the electronic telegraph and its modern incarnations are your friend.

Now, some may tell you that attempting to use alcohol in a cooked dish is a waste of time, and that all the good stuff will evaporate off long before it reaches your palate. Well, opinion is divided on the issue – and this tome certainly contains weak as well as strong dishes – but the Angels must have their share, and if you feel hard done by, slosh in a little more.

To those who say such a concentration on the products

of fermentation and distillation – surely God's greatest gifts to man – are injurious to health, I can only say that I am long in the tooth, and blue in the conk, but none of them have done me any harm. Life is short, and the time between good meals is longer than it needs to be. Enjoy such fruits while you may, and do take care of my cat.

Yours,

The Right Hon. George Harvey Bone, Esq.
London, October 2007

WINE

"It is well to remember that there are five reasons for drinking: the arrival of a friend; one's present or future thirst; the excellence of the wine; or any other reason."
Ancient Latin saying

COQ AU VIN

Coq au Vin is the granddaddy of boozy dishes. A whole bottle of wine. Do it right, and this is probably the best recipe in the book. Serves 4 hungry people, and fills them right up.

1 large chicken
whole black pepper
150g (5 oz) bacon, cut into thin strips
butter
2 medium onions, roughly chopped
1 large carrot, roughly chopped
2 cloves of garlic
2 tbsps plain flour
4 or 5 small sprigs of thyme
3 bay leaves
80g (3 oz) butter
12 shallots, peeled
200g small mushrooms
2 tbsps cognac
a bottle of red wine

For the stock:
1 large onion, roughly chopped
1 large carrot, roughly chopped
whole black pepper

Joint the chicken into 6 or 8 pieces, and put the giblets, carcass and bones into a large pan with one of the onions and one of the carrots, a dozen or so peppercorns, and cover with water. Bring it to the boil then turn down the heat and leave to simmer.

In a large casserole pot, cook the bacon strips with half the butter over a medium heat for 1-2 minutes. Take the strips out, set them aside, and cook the chicken pieces in the hot fat, packed together and turning them over when they start to brown. Take the chicken out and put with the bacon.

Cook the onions, carrot and garlic in the same pan for a few minutes, until the onion softens, then put the chicken and the bacon back in and stir in the flour. Cook for a couple of minutes more, then stick in the thyme and bay leaves and slosh in the wine and cognac. Spoon in the hot stock until everything is covered, and bring to the boil. Immediately turn it down and allow to simmer.

Melt the rest of the butter in a small pan, and cook the shallots and mushrooms for 5 minutes. Add these to the chicken pot and leave simmering for 45 minutes to an hour – check that the chicken is good and tender.

Finally, take the chicken out and boil the sauce to thicken it up a little, but not too much. A few minutes should do the trick. Put the chicken back in and serve.

CONYNGS IN GREKE WINE

Conyng is an Old English world meaning coney or rabbit, and this dish has existed in our land since at least the fourteenth century. Indeed, this dish was one of the main courses at the coronation of Henry IV in 1399. Excellent served with rice for 4 people.

1 rabbit, portioned
olive oil
3 tbsps red wine vinegar

For the marinade:
170g (6 oz) Muscatel raisins (seedless)
170g (6 oz) dried apricots
3 large pieces ginger, sliced
1 tbsp syrup from the stem ginger
1 tsp ground ginger
1 tsp ground cinnamon
1 tsp ground cloves
12 juniper berries (optional)
250ml (1/2 pint) sweet Greek red wine or white wine

Seasoned flour (vary according to what you have):
150 (5 oz) flour
1 tbsp salt
1/2 tbsp celery salt
1/2 tbsp pepper
1 tbsp dry mustard
2 tbsp paprika
1 tbsp garlic powder
1 tsp ginger

1/4 tsp thyme
1/4 tsp sweet basil
1/4 tsp oregano

Put all the ingredients for the marinade in a large bowl, cover and leave overnight to blend. The next day, arrange the rabbit portions on a dish and pour over the marinated fruit and wine. Leave for at least 5 or 6 hours, then remove the rabbit portions and dry them.

Coat the pieces in the seasoned flour and fry until golden in gently smoking oil. Drain off excess oil. Pour over the fruit marinade, and cover and simmer for 30-40 minutes, or until the largest parts are tender (the back fillets will be cooked first).

Remove the rabbit pieces and keep warm while you reduce the sauce until thick and cohered, by boiling rapidly for 10-15 minutes, then recombine and serve.

PATATAS A LA RIOJANA

To make this spicy tapas dish truly authentic, use a good white Rioja, although any good quality dry white will do.

> 650g (1 1/2 lbs) small potatoes
> 175ml (1/3 cup) olive oil
> 1 large onion, sliced
> 2 garlic cloves, finely chopped
> 2 red peppers, chopped
> 1 tbsp paprika
> 1 tsp salt
> 225g (1/2 lb) chorizo, sliced
> water
> 2-3 guindillas or other small mildly hot pickled chile
>   peppers
> 125 ml (1/2 cup) dry white wine

Cut the potatoes halfway through, and then snap them open to produce fluffy and absorbent edges. Cook them in hot oil in a large pan for 10 minutes or so, until golden brown. Add the onion and garlic and keep stirring until the onion is soft. Stir in the red peppers, paprika and salt and cook for a further two minutes. Stir in the chorizo and the wine and allow to reduce for a few minutes, then cover with water and add the chillies. Bring to the boil, then reduce heat and simmer for 15 minutes, until the potatoes are tender. Remove the chillies and ladle into bowls. Serve with salad and bread.

RIBS BRAISED IN WINE

"If God forbade drinking, would He have made wine so good?"—Cardinal Richelieu

> 8 short ribs, trimmed of excess fat
> 2 tbsp vegetable oil
> 1 tbsp plain flour
> 10 cloves garlic, peeled
> 8 large shallots, peeled and split
> 2 medium carrots, peeled and quartered
> 2 stalks celery, peeled, and cut into small pieces
> 1 medium leek, washed and roughly chopped
> 6 sprigs parsley
> 2 sprigs thyme
> 2 bay leaves
> 2 tbsp tomato paste
> 2.8l (3 quarts) stock
> Freshly ground white pepper
> 3 bottles dry red wine

Preheat the oven to 180C/350F/Gas Mark 4. Pour the wine into a large a saucepan and heat. When it's hot, light it carefully, allow to burn out, then boil. Keep boiling until the wine has reduced by half, then remove from the heat.

Heat the oil in a large casserole dish. Season the ribs with salt and black pepper, and dust with flour. Sear the ribs in the hot oil for 4 to 5 minutes on each side. Set the browned ribs aside, remove all but 1 tbsp of the fat from the pan, and toss in the garlic, shallots, carrots, celery, leeks, parsley, thyme and bay leaves. Cook these for about 5 minutes, until they begin to soften and brown, then spoon in the tomato paste and stir for a minute to mix well.

Pour the reduced wine into the pot, as well as the stock, and put the ribs back in. Bring to the boil, then cover and place on the middle shelf of the oven for 2 1/2 hours, or until the ribs are tender enough to be easily skewered. Skim the mixture of excess fat every 30 minutes or so.

After cooking, put the meat to one side and boil the liquid in the pan to reduce it further. Season to taste, and strain out the solids. Serve with vegetables, pouring the sauce over the ribs and sprinkling with celery.

MOULES À LA MARINIÈRE

The best use of bad wine is to drive away poor relations, they say. Well, this serves 4, so get out the good stuff.

> 1.8kg (4 lbs) mussels
> 4 shallots, finely chopped
> 4 garlic cloves, finely chopped
> 1 tbsp plain flour
> 2 big handfuls fresh parsley, roughly chopped
> 6 tbsp butter, cut into pieces
> 500ml (1 pint) dry white wine

Fry the shallots and garlic gently with some parsley stalks until soft, then add the flour and stir well. Pour in the wine, and bring to the boil, stirring all the time to avoid lumps. Once boiling, add the mussels (clean them first, removing barnacles and beards – and don't cook any that stay open when you wash them). Boil for three to four minutes, covered, shaking the pot from time to time. They're cooked when they're all (or almost all) open. Stir in the butter and parsley and serve with plenty of good french bread.

ALL-IN-ONE GUINEAFOWL

This fantastic dish includes everything you need for a full roast dinner in one pan, so it's not much work, and the gamey guineafowl gives it plenty of flavour. Serves several hungry people.

1 guineafowl
3-4 large sprigs rosemary, chopped
2 cloves garlic, finely chopped
2 fennel bulbs, quartered,
2 large red onions, quartered
450g (1 lb) small new potatoes
3 tbsp pancetta, cubed
2 tbsp olive oil
salt and pepper
large glass white wine

Preheat the oven to 200C/400F/Gas Mark 6. Take the guineafowl and chop it into four or eight chunks. Mix the rosemary and garlic with the oil and season with salt and pepper, then rub over the guineafowl. Place in a large roasting dish and pack the fennel, onions and potatoes in tight around it, tossing the lot to coat everything in oil. Sprinkle with the pancetta for extra flavour. Roast in the oven for half an hour, then slosh over the wine and cook for a further 15 minutes.

HUÎTRES AU CHAMPAGNE

This recipe was allegedly created at the Hôtel de la Côte d'Or in Saulieu, near Dijon, by the legendary chef-patron Monsieur François Minot. I cannot add any more – except more champagne. Serves 6-8.

> 48 flat, round oysters
> 1 shallot, chopped
> 4 large egg yolks
> 225g (8 oz) butter
> 250ml (1/2 pint) thick, whipped cream
> 1/2 bottle champagne

Shuck the oysters and put them with their liquid in a large pan, arranging the shells on a baking tray. Boil the wine and shallot until there's barely a tablespoon of liquid left. Cool to tepid, beat in the egg yolks, then return the pan to a low heat and add butter bit by bit to make a hollandaise sauce. When very thick, fold in the whipped cream and season. Put oysters over the heat for a few seconds until they turn opaque and stiffen slightly. Return them to their shells, cover with the sauce, and brown under the grill. Swallow.

CLAMS IN PROSECCO

This is a very modern Italian dish. Although you can make it with champagne or other sparkling wine, the nutty bitterness of prosecco is the best choice.

>320g (11 oz) spaghetti
>3kg (6 1/2 lbs) small clams, well washed
>3 cloves garlic, crushed
>2 tbsp parsley leaves, roughly chopped
>2 dried chillies, finely chopped
>3 tbsp olive oil
>2 lemons
>250ml (1/2 pint) prosecco

Heat the olive oil in a thick-bottomed pan, and cook the garlic until it starts to brown. Chuck in the chilli, clams and Prosecco, then cover and cook on a high heat for three minutes or so to open the clams (chuck out those that don't open). Season to taste and keep warm while you cook the spaghetti.

Cook the spaghetti and add to the sauce, mixing it all together over a high heat. Pick out any empty shells and add some parsley and lemon before serving.

WINE

VIN SANTO AND PROSCIUTTO

Vin Santo, an Italian dessert wine, got its name from a Siennese legend which tells of a Franciscan friar who in 1348 cured plague victims with the wine normally used by the brothers to celebrate the mass; the conviction that this wine had miraculous properties spread, leading to the epithet *santo* ('holy'). This dish is pretty blessed too.

> 250g (9 oz) risotto rice
> 8 slices prosciutto
> 1 red onion, finely chopped
> 1 celery head, chopped
> 100g (4 oz) parmesan, grated
> 1.5l (3 pints) chicken stock
> 200g (7 oz) butter
> 350ml (3/4 pint) Vin Santo

Bring the stock to a simmer and season. Melt half the butter in a thick-bottomed saucepan and gently fry the onion and celery until soft and beginning to colour. Add the rice and stir to coat all the grains. Add 250ml of the Vin Santo and stir until it's been absorbed, then start to slowly add the stock, spoonful by spoonful, until it's all been absorbed and the rice is cooked—this takes about twenty minutes. Remove from the heat and stir in the remaining Vin Santo, the butter and parmesan, and serve with thin slices of prosciutto.

KING PRAWNS IN SAKE

The first sake, Japanese rice wine, was made by people chewing rice, chestnuts, millet and acorn and spitting the mixture into a tub. Luckily, production has moved on somewhat since those times, and the only mouth this lot is going in will be yours. Serves 4.

650g (1 1/2 lb) king prawns
2 pears, peeled, cored and chopped
125ml (1/2 cup) sweet chilli sauce
noodles

Marinade the prawns in the sake for several hours, and preferably overnight. Fry the pears in a little oil until soft, then add the prawns and cook for a few minutes. Mix in the chilli sauce, heat through, and serve with noodles.

CHAMPAGNE AND VEGETABLE SOUP

"Remember gentlemen, it's not just France we are fighting for, it's Champagne!"—Winston Churchill

330g (12 oz) peas (fresh is best, frozen will do)
1 carrot, finely chopped
1 medium onion, finely chopped
1 bay leaf
pinch sage, chervil, and thyme
750ml (1 1/2 pints) stock
1 teaspoon fresh lemon juice
250g (9 oz) whipping cream
125ml (1/4 pint) dry sherry
250ml (1/2 pint) brut champagne

In a large pan, combine the peas, carrot, onion and herbs. Cover with water and simmer until the peas are very soft. Remove and discard the carrot, onion and bay leaves. Blend or mash the remaining liquid until smooth. Return to the heat and add the stock, sherry and lemon juice, and salt and pepper to taste. Whip the cream to stiff peaks, bring the liquid to the boil and fold in the cream. Remove from the heat, add the champagne, and serve immediately in warm bowls. Serves 6.

WINE SOUP

"O thou invisible spirit of wine, if thou hast no name to be known by, let us call thee devil."—William Shakespeare (it should be noted that dear old Bill was not talking about this soup, which should serve 2 with no ill effects).

> 3 egg yolks
> 1 tsp plain flour
> 1 tsp sugar
> 175ml (1/3 pint) water
> 350ml (1/2 a bottle) white wine

Beat 3 yolks of quite fresh eggs to a froth with a whisk over the fire, adding a small teaspoonful each of fine flour and white sugar, half a bottle of white wine, and half that quantity of water. Whisk till it comes to the boil, then take it off and serve immediately, before the froth subsides.

CLARET JELLY

"How I like claret! ... It fills one's mouth with a gushing freshness, then goes down to cool and feverless; then, you do not feel it quarreling with one's liver. No; 'tis rather a peace-maker, and lies as quiet as it did in the grape. Then it is as fragrant as the Queen Bee, and the more ethereal part mounts into the brain, not assaulting the cerebral apartments, like a bully looking for his trull, and hurrying from door to door, bouncing against the wainscott, but rather walks like Aladdin about his enchanted palace, so gently that you do not feel his step."—John Keats

> *4 lemons (125ml / 1/4 pint juice)*
> *600ml (1 1/4 pints) water*
> *170g (6 oz) sugar*
> *40g (1 1/2 oz) gelatine*
> *whites and crushed shells of two eggs*
> *carmine*
> *125ml (1/4 pt) claret*

Thinly cut the lemon rinds and mix with water, sugar and gelatine. Add crushed shells and whites of eggs and the lemon juice. Heat slowly, whisking all the time until nearly boiling, then stop whisking and allow to boil. Pour in the claret without disturbing the foam 'crust'. Boil again to the top of the pan, then remove from the heat, cover, and leave to settle for a minute. Filter the results through a cloth, cool, add the colouring, remove the froth and place in 4-6 individual moulds in the fridge for about an hour to set.

FORTIFIED WINES

"Port is not for the very young, the vain and the active. It
is the comfort of age and the companion of the scholar
and the philosopher."
Evelyn Waugh

CHRISTMAS PUDDING

No single dish is closer to the heart of the boozy gourmand than Christmas Pud, with its mouth-watering combinations of fruits and lashings of alcohol.

The art of the Christmas Pudding has declined in recent years with the advent of the store-bought, or pre-prepared version, which is almost universally lacking in sufficient texture, moisture and alcoholic content. At Bone Towers, Mother produces this version every Christmas, and after a month locked in the scullery agreed to share her secrets.

Prepare at least four weeks before Christmas – preferably on Stir-up Sunday, the last Sunday before Advent: "Stir up, we beseech thee, O Lord, the wills of thy faithful people". This version will serve 8-10 people.

> 225g (8 oz) stoned muscatels or other raisins
> 225g (8 oz) currants
> 170g (6 oz) brown bread crumbs
> 55g (2 oz) blanched almonds chopped
> 55g (2 oz) glacé cherries quartered
> 55g (2 oz) light muscovado sugar
> 2 tbsp grated orange/tangerine zest
> 1 tsp ground cinnamon
> 1 tsp freshly grated nutmeg
> 1/4 tsp ground cloves
> 3 large eggs
> 125ml (1/4 pint) port
> 6 tbsps brandy

Put all the dry ingredients in a large bowl. Whisk together all the liquids, then pour over the dry ingredients and mix well. Butter a pudding basin, and line with buttered, grease-proof paper. Pour in the mixture to fill the bowl, and cover with more grease-proof paper or foil. Place in a large saucepan on a couple of eggcups or similar, pour in a few inches of water and steam for 5 hours.

Once steamed, feed the pudding with a couple more tbsp of brandy before removing from the pot and putting the bowl away in a cool dry place. On Christmas day, steam for a further two hours before serving.

To serve, warm a large slug of brandy in a pan, mixed with a tbsp of vodka to get a nice blue flavour. Place the pud on a warm plate (this keeps the flame going longer) and, igniting the warm brandy and vodka, pour it over the top. Serve with brandy butter.

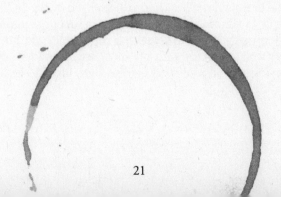

NO ORDINARY CHICKEN PIE

1 chicken (1.8 kg / 4 lb)
100g (4 oz) mushrooms, washed and sliced
100g (4 oz) liver pâté
3 egg yolks
80g (3 oz) butter
2 tbsp plain flour
3 cloves
pinch thyme
2 bay leaves
225g (8 oz) flaky pastry
3 tbsp sherry

Put the chicken in a saucepan with sufficient water to cover it, add herbs and seasoning then simmer for 30-50 minutes or until flesh comes easily off the bone. Remove from the heat. While chicken is cooling, sauté mushrooms in half the butter. Strain the stock from the chicken pot into a jug. Bone chicken and remove the skin, cutting the flesh into small pieces and placing in a pie dish.

Make sauce by heating 750ml (1 1/2 pint) stock with the rest of the butter, mixing in the flour. Bring to the boil then remove heat and stir in sherry. Tip a little of the stock onto the egg yolks in a bowl and mix thoroughly. When the stock has cooled a little stir in the egg yolks together with the mushrooms and pâté. Add seasoning and pour over chicken. Allow to chill overnight in fridge.

Next day cover with pastry and bake in the oven at 180C/350F/Gas Mark 4 for about 30 minutes, until the pastry is nicely brown on top.

GRANDMA DORSET'S TRIFLE

This is my grandmother's trifle, subtitled 'The Real Thing'. Small children and those of a weak constitution should not be allowed anywhere near it, and even those made of stronger stuff may have trouble getting up from the table at the end of the meal. You have been warned.

> *3 small sponge cakes*
> *6-8 macaroons*
> *a little grated lemon rind*
> *28g (1 oz) almonds, blanched and roughly chopped*
> *strawberry jam*
> *250ml (1/2 pint) custard*
> *125ml (1/4 pint) sherry*
> *3 tbsp brandy*
>
> *For the whip:*
> *125ml (1/4 pint) cream*
> *1 tbsp sugar*
> *1 egg white*
> *1 tsp sherry*

Put the sponge cake and macaroons in a bowl. Pour over the sherry and the brandy, then add the lemon rind, almonds and jam. Pour over cold custard. Beat the whip ingredients in a bowl and spoon over the top. Garnish with whatever you have to hand – cherries, more nuts, chocolate. It's up to you.

MARSALA ICE CREAM

Fortified Marsala wine was first popularised by English trader John Woodhouse who landed at the Sicilian port in 1773 and fell in love with its strong flavour.

In England, Woodhouse discovered that Marsala wine was such a hit that he returned to Sicily and, in 1796, began the mass production and commercialisation of the drink. Woodhouse himself became notorious in the area as he would often consume copious amounts of Marsala, and while in an inebriated state would run naked through the vineyards. You might be safer sticking with this gorgeous ice cream.

> 10 egg yolks
> 200g (7 oz) caster sugar
> 450ml (1 pint) double cream
> 350ml (3/4 pint) dry marsala

Beat the sugar into the yolks until light and fluffy. Add a third of the Marsala and transfer to a bowl that will sit comfortably on a pan of simmering water – without touching the water. Keep stirring over half an hour while the mixture comes to the boil, then stir in the remaining Marsala and allow to cool.

Beat the cream then fold it into the mixture. Stick it in the freezer, stirring every half hour or so until it has frozen completely.

PORT JELLY

"I have often thought that the aim of port is to give you a good and durable hangover, so that during the next day you should be reminded of the splendid occasion the night before."—George Mikes

> 500ml (1 pint) water
> 55g (2 oz) sugar
> 2 tbsp redcurrant jelly
> 28g (1 oz) gelatine
> cochineal
> 250ml (1/2 pt) port wine

Put water, sugar, redcurrant jelly and gelatine into a pan and leave to soak for 5 minutes, then heat slowly until dissolved. Add half the port wine and colour red with a few drops of cochineal. Strain through double muslin; add the rest of the wine then pour into a wet mould or bowl. Should set in a couple of hours in the fridge.

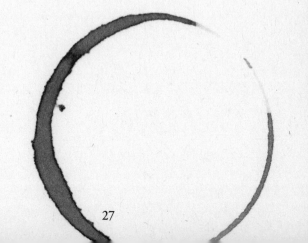

BEER

"24 hours in a day, 24 beers in a case. Coincidence?"
Stephen Wright

MEXICAN DRUNK CHICKEN

Pollo En Pulque, to give it its proper name, is a Tex-Mex staple. Serves 8.

> 4 chicken breasts with skin on
> 4 leg quarters with skin on
> 2 tbsp olive oil
> 1 small white onion, peeled
> 3 cloves garlic, crushed
> 350ml (3/4 pint) chicken stock
> 1 large very ripe tomato, diced
> 1 large fresh chilli pepper, chopped
> 1 tsp allspice
> 1/2 cinnamon
> 10 small potatoes
> 1 can medium-dark beer

Preheat the oven to 375F/190C/Gas Mark 5. In a medium pan, sauté the onion and garlic in the oil until soft. Pour this into a large casserole dish and place the chicken on top. Add the beer, stock, tomato, chillies, allspice, cinnamon and a pinch of salt.

Cover the dish, and place the casserole in the oven and bake for 30 minutes. Add the whole potatoes and put back for another 30 minutes, then finally uncover and cook for another 15 minutes, until browned on top. Serve with rice.

BEER & ONION SOUP

A personal favourite this. A dark ale works best – I usually use Guinness ale (not stout) – but anything flavoursome will do. Serves a couple of hungry people.

> *4 large onions, sliced*
> *50g (2 oz) butter*
> *500ml (1 pint) bouillon or vegetable stock*
> *half a baguette, halved*
> *200g (7 oz) cheddar cheese, grated*
> *pinch sugar*
> *half a bottle of beer*

Melt the butter in a large pan and fry the onions on a low heat for a good half an hour, adding the sugar after about ten minutes to help the onion caramelise – this is very important. When they're browned and sticking to the pan, add the bouillon or stock and the beer, and simmer for another thirty minutes.

When nearly ready to serve, lightly toast both sides of the baguette halves, then sprinkle the cheese on the inner sides and grill until bubbling. Place as much of these as you can fit into large bowls, then spoon the soup over to serve.

BEER BRATS

"You can't be a real country unless you have a beer and an airline – it helps if you have some kind of a football team, or some nuclear weapons, but at the very least you need a beer."—Frank Zappa

> 2 teaspoons olive oil
> 1 large onion, sliced into rings
> 6 bratwurst sausages
> half a can of beer

Heat half the oil in a large pan and brown the sausages. Remove them from the pan, add the rest of the olive oil, and cook the onion rings in the fat. Cook, stirring constantly, until soft and clear but not brown. Return the bratwurst to the pan and add the beer, cooking over a medium heat until the beer has cooked down to a thick sauce, about 10 to 15 minutes. Serve in a bun.

BEER BATTER

Beer batter is great for battering everything from classic fish and chips and onion rings to delicate Japanese tempura vegetables. Just coat whatever you like and deep fry.

300g (10 oz) plain flour
1 1/2 tsp baking powder
1 tsp salt
1/2 tsp pepper
2 eggs
500ml (1/2 pint) beer

Sift the flour into a large bowl, and mix in the baking powder, salt and pepper. Make a well in the centre of the mix and break in one egg at a time, whisking until absorbed. Then gradually add the beer, whisking constantly to form a smooth batter.

BEER BUTT CHICKEN

This strange but wonderful barbecue dish involves placing a can of beer into the cavity of a chicken and roasting it. The beer boils inside the can, forcing flavour out and through the meat.

> 1 chicken (About 1.5kg or 3 1/2 lbs)
> 2 tbsp of your favourite barbecue rub
> 2 tbsp vegetable oil
> 1 can beer

Open and drink about a third of the beer, then make a couple of extra holes in the top. Remove the giblets and fat from the inside of the chicken and wash and dry well. Sprinkle a little of the rub on the inside of the chicken, brush the outside with the oil, sprinkle most of the rub over the bird, and put the last bit in the beer can (watch out for it foaming up).

Hold the bird upright, and insert the can as far as possible into the cavity. Place very carefully on the grill, sitting the bird on the base of the beer can, and balance with the chicken's legs to form a tripod. Tuck the wings behind and cover to cook for 1 1/4 to 1 1/2 hours. Check regularly – if the skin is browning too much, wrap in aluminium foil.

When cooked – check it really is all the way through, set aside for five minutes to cool then remove the can, taking care of the hot beer. Carve and serve.

BIERBROOD

South African Beer Bread. This is great with soup on a cold winter's night.

> *500g self-raising flour*
> *125g cheddar cheese*
> *50ml sesame or sunflower seeds*
> *3 tbsp castor sugar*
> *1/2 tsp salt*
> *330ml beer*

Pre-heat the oven to 180C/350F/Gas Mark 4. Grease a small loaf tin and sift flour, sugar and salt together in a mixing bowl. Then stir in the cheese and beer – you can add a little water if the dough is still too dry. You need to mix it until all the flour has been moistened and the dough forms a single, sticky lump in the bowl. Press this gently into the loaf tin, sprinkle with seeds, and place in the warm oven. After about an hour it should be nicely brown on the top – stick a skewer in, and if it comes out clean, it's done. Let it cool and serve with plenty of butter.

CHINESE BEER CHICKEN

Some people eat a hot curry and drink a beer with it. Why bother? With Chinese Beer Chicken you can get two-in-one. Serves 2.

> 2 chicken breasts
> 2 spring onions, finely chopped
> 2 tbsp soy sauce
> 2 cloves garlic, finely chopped
> 2 tsp dried chilli
> 2 tsp ginger, chopped
> 1 tsp cornflour
> pinch of sugar
> 200ml beer (plus a little extra)

Mix half the garlic, the soy sauce, cornflour and a dash of beer and marinate the chicken in it for at least a couple of hours. Cook the rest of the garlic, the spring onion and the ginger in a little oil until they begin to soften, then add the chicken to stir-fry. When it begins to cook, add some more soy sauce and the sugar, and when that's evaporated, pour over the beer. When that's evaporated too, you're done. Serve with rice.

POTATO SALAD WITH BEER DRESSING

"I would kill everyone in this room for a drop of sweet beer."—Homer J. Simpson

> 1 kg (2 1/2 lbs) potatoes
> 1 large red onion, roughly chopped
> 3 tbsp parsley, finely chopped
> 2 tbsp chives, chopped
>
> For the dressing:
> 6 tbsp olive oil
> 1 medium onion, finely chopped
> 3 tbsp malt or cider vinegar
> 1 tbsp Dijon mustard
> 1/2 tsp sugar
> 250ml (1/2 pint) lager

To make the dressing cook the onion in 2 tbsp oil until soft, then add the beer, vinegar and sugar and boil for 5 minutes. Add the mustard and whisk hard, and continue whisking while you add the remaining oil. Set aside to blend while you cook the potatoes.

Cook the potatoes in boiling water for about 20 minutes, until they slide off a knife. Remove and drain, and as soon as you can handle them, cut them, unpeeled, into thumb-sized pieces. While still warm, toss them gently in the onion, parsley and dressing and garnish with the chives.

BEERY CHEESE SPREAD

This is lovely with some toasted pitta or tortilla chips. And a beer.

> 2 cups cheddar cheese, finely grated
> 1/4 cup beer
> 3 tablespoons tomato purée
> 2 tsp Lea & Perrins
> 1 clove garlic, crushed

Make sure the cheese has been out of the fridge for a while so it's not all hard, then put it into a bowl with the beer, the tomato paste, the Lea & Perrins and the garlic. Blend or whisk with a fork as hard as you can, then leave it to soak for at least a couple of hours – or better, overnight. Then pile it on.

STOUT AND SPICY PASTA

Guinness dishes are usually pretty heavy, but this one packs an unexpected punch. Smoked chillies (chipotles) are best, but regular jalapeños will do. Serves 4-6.

3 tbsp cooking oil
680g (1.5 lbs) chicken breasts, cut into bite-sized pieces
1 medium onion, finely diced
8 garlic cloves, crushed
2 1/2 tsp salt
1/2 tsp pepper
2 tins chopped tomatoes, drained
1 tin (150ml) tomato paste
2 tbsp sugar
1 tbsp dried oregano
1 tbsp dried thyme
2 fresh large red chillies, finely chopped
440ml can Guinness (or other dark stout)
375g pasta
Fresh parsley, chopped fine, for garnish

Cook the chicken breasts in the oil over a medium-high heat until browned and cooked all the way through. Lift them out, turn it down a bit, and cook the onions and garlic in the same pan for 2 to 3 minutes, stirring occasionally, until soft. Stir in the tomatoes, tomato paste, sugar, herbs and chillies, pour in the beer and bring to the boil. Once boiling, reduce the heat and let the sauce thicken for about five minutes. Cook the pasta while this is happening, and when all is ready, mix the chicken back into the sauce and serve immediately.

SCOTCH ALE SPUDS

These dark and beery potatoes work well on a barbecue or in a hot oven, and are great with lamb, in particular. Serves 4.

4 large potatoes
2 tbsp oil
twigs of fresh rosemary
4 shallots, finely chopped
1/2 can dark Scottish ale

Mix the ale, oil, shallots and rosemary in a bowl. Chop the potatoes into thumb-sized chunks, and toss them in the mixture, coating them well. Leave to soak for at least an hour, then pick out the spuds onto a sheet of foil. Drizzle a little of the marinade over them, then wrap tightly and place on a BBQ grill or in a hot oven for 40 minutes or so.

SOUTHERN COOKED GREENS

"I'd rather have a bottle in front of me, than a frontal lobotomy."—Tom Waits

> 225g (1/2 lb) raw bacon, chopped
> 3 medium onions, roughly chopped
> pinch cayenne pepper
> 2 shallots, finely chopped
> 2 cloves garlic, crushed
> 75ml (1/4 cup) white wine vinegar
> 1 tbsp brown sugar
> 3 kg (6 lbs) greens, collard greens, kale, or spinach, washed and stemmed
> 1 330ml bottle beer

In a large pot, fry the bacon until crispy. Add the onions and cook until soft. Season with salt, pepper, and cayenne. Add the shallots and garlic and cook for two minutes, then stir in the beer, vinegar and brown sugar. Add the greens a portion at time, pressing down as they wilt to provide room for the next bunch. Cook uncovered for about an hour.

BEER PUFFS

These puffs can be filled with any filling of your choice – pâté, tuna salad, seafood, cheese or vegetables all work. This makes 60 to 80 small puffs.

> 110g (4 oz) butter
> 150g (5 oz) plain flour, sifted
> 1/2 tsp salt
> 4 eggs
> filling of your choice
> 250ml (1/2 pint) beer

Preheat the oven to 230C/450F/Gas Mark 8. Butter a baking tray well. In a heavy saucepan, melt the butter into the beer and heat until it just starts to boil. Add the flour and salt gradually, stirring constantly until the mixture thickens and starts to form a ball. Remove from the heat and leave to stand for 1 minute. Add the eggs one at a time, beating each one in until the dough is shiny.

Drop the dough onto the baking tray in 2cm (1 inch) balls. Bake the balls in the oven for 10 minutes, then reduce the heat to 180C/350F/Gas Mark 4 and bake for another 10 minutes until brown and dry.

Allow the puffs to cool for some time in a dry place, then split them open and fill with your filling of choice.

CIDER

"He that drinks his cider alone,
let him catch his horse alone."
Benjamin Franklin

ROAST PORK WITH APPLE STUFFING AND CIDER SAUCE

Quite an undertaking this one, but there's nothing quite like roast pork with apple sauce – particularly of the more boozy variety. This way, the apple sauce cooks in the pan with the roast.

1/2 tbsp olive oil
1/2 tbsp butter
1 small onion, finely chopped
2 garlic cloves, crushed
1 tbsp minced fresh chives
1 tbsp minced fresh parsley
1/2 tbsp fresh sage
1/2 tbsp fresh thyme
1 large, tart apple, peeled and chopped into 1cm (1/2 in) pieces
180ml (3/4 cup) breadcrumbs
80ml (1/3 cup) cider

For the roast:
1.8kg (4 lb) boneless pork roast, cut lengthwise, three-quarters of the way through the middle but not all the way through
1 1/2 tbsp fresh sage, finely chopped
1 1/2 tbsp fresh rosemary, finely chopped
9 garlic cloves, 8 left whole and 1 thinly sliced
3 tart apples, peeled, cored and cut into 6 wedges each
375ml (1 1/2 cups) cider

To make the stuffing, heat the oil and butter over a low heat and fry the onion and garlic until soft, with a little salt and pepper. Stir in the chives, parsley, sage and thyme and cook for one minute. Add the chopped apple and cook for another four minutes, until the apples start to soften. Remove from the heat and stir in the bread-crumbs and cider and season.

Preheat the oven to 230C/450F/Gas Mark 8. Open the meat up and season both sides with salt and pepper. Sprinkle a quarter of the sage and rosemary on each side. Spread the stuffing evenly over one side and tie tightly closed with several lengths of string. Place the meat, fat side up, in a roasting pan. Score several large Xs in the fat side and insert the thinly sliced garlic. Place the apple wedges around the meat and pour the cider over everything. Sprinkle with salt, pepper and the remaining sage and rosemary.

Roast for 15 minutes then reduce to 200C/400F/Gas Mark 6 for a further hour, basting once or twice. Let the roast sit for 5 or 10 minutes before removing the string and slicing. Spoon the sauce over to serve.

SAUSAGES IN CIDER

Sausages and mash with extra apple-based goodness. Serves 4.

> 450g (1 lb) – about 8 – fat, coarse ground pork or beef sausages
> 450g (1 lb) onions, peeled and cut in rough chunks
> 1 tsp English mustard
> a pinch of thyme
> 1 large red apple, cored but not peeled, in 8-10 slices.
> 250ml (1/2 pint) cider

Prick the sausages with a fork, and lightly brown them in a heavy pan for about 5 minutes, turning often. The pan should be just big enough, because you want to pack the ingredients in tightly. Pack the onions around the sausages and stir in the mustard, thyme and cider. Cover and simmer over medium heat for half an hour, being careful not to let it boil. The juices will form a rich gravy. Place the apple slices on top and cover and simmer for another five minutes until softened. Serve with a generous portion of mashed potato.

MATELOTE NORMANDE

One from the Bone's farmhouse in Normandy this one – feel free to substitute red wine for the cider, and eau de vie or even whisky for the Calvados. This, however, is the real thing. Serves 6.

> 900g (2 lb) fish – 225g (1/2 lb) conger eel, and a mixture of plaice, dabs, whiting and gurnard, all cleaned and cut into strips.
> 80g (3 oz) butter
> liquor from mussels
> 250ml (1/2 pint) fish or light meat stock
> 110g (4 oz) thick cream
> 1 tbsp butter
> 1 tbsp plain flour
> 1 tbsp chervil, chopped
> 2 - 4 tbsp Calvados
> 250ml (1/2 pt) dry cider
>
> For the garnish:
> 1/2 lb mushrooms, lightly fried
> 2 pints mussels, opened
> croûtons of bread fried in butter

Cook the fish in the butter until the pieces are very lightly coloured. Pour over the warmed calvados, set it alight, and stir the fish about in the flames. Add cider, mussel liquor and stock. Season with salt and pepper and add some chopped chervil. Simmer until the fish is just cooked.

Add the butter and flour mashed together in small lumps to thicken, then pour in the cream. Don't let it boil, just thicken gently over a medium heat.

Transfer the lot to a warm serving dish and arrange the mushrooms, mussels and croûtons around the fish.

CIDER DOUGHNUTS

Ah, the gilded days of my youth. The green fields of Somerset, tending to yellow, and the golden cider gleaming in the glass. Nanny would give us half a pint with breakfast, and make these doughnuts for our tea. Such beautiful, blurry days. This recipe makes a dozen.

> 500g (18 oz) plus 2 tbsp plain flour
> 1 tbsp baking powder
> 1 tsp baking soda
> 1 tsp powdered buttermilk
> 3/4 tsp cinnamon
> 1/2 tsp salt
> 50g (2 oz) butter, melted
> 2 large eggs, beaten
> 125g (5 oz) sugar
> 1 tsp vanilla extract
> 1 litre (4 pints) vegetable oil for frying
> 250ml (1/2 pint) cider
>
> For dusting:
> 1 tbsp cinnamon
> 400g (15 oz) sugar

For the batter, mix the flour, baking powder, baking soda, powdered buttermilk, cinnamon and salt in a large bowl. In another bowl, mix the cider and melted butter. In a third bowl whisk together the eggs, sugar and vanilla in a large bowl until thick. Using a wooden spoon, add the flour and cider mixtures in alternate spoonfuls to the egg mixture until well mixed.

Cover the bowl with clingfilm and put it in the fridge for at least an hour.

When chilled, turn the dough out onto a well-floured surface and roll out to about 20mm (3/4 inch) thick. A 75mm (3 inch) doughnut cutter is perfect for the next, but if you don't have this you can make the rings by hand – they should be about that diameter, with a good space in the middle, and well joined. Place on a tray and chill for a good half hour.

Fry the doughnuts by heating about 10cm (4 inches) of vegetable oil in a large, deep pan over a medium-high heat. Fry the doughnuts in batches of three or so (depending on pan size) for about 2 minutes on each side, until golden. Remove with a slotted spoon and drain on a wire rack. Place the dusting cinnamon and sugar in a closed container and shake well. When the doughnuts have cooled, place them one at a time in the container and shake gently to coat. Then stuff yourself.

CIDER CUPCAKES

Mmmmmmmm. Cupcakes. Makes 18.

For the cupcakes:
200g (7 oz) butter
200g (7 oz) sugar
2 large eggs
300g (10 oz) plain flour, sifted
1/8 tsp ground cloves
1 tsp cinnamon
1 tsp baking soda
750ml (1 1/2 pints) cider

For the icing:
500ml (1 pint) cider
170g (6 oz) cream cheese
65g (2 1/4 oz) icing sugar

Preheat the oven to 190C/375F/Gas Mark 5. In a large saucepan, boil the cider until it has reduced by half, and let it cool. In a bowl, beat the butter and sugar until fluffy and add the eggs one at a time, beating them in well. Sift in the flour, cloves, cinnamon baking soda, a pinch of salt, the reduced cider and mix well. Divide the batter into 18 paper-lined muffin tins and bake for 25 minutes, or until a skewer poked into one of the cakes comes out clean. Allow to cool, then remove from the tins.

For the icing, again boil the cider – this time, down to about 125ml (1/4 pint) and let it cool. Mix the cream cheese, icing sugar, cider and a pinch of salt in a bowl and beat together. Spread the icing on the cupcakes, and gorge.

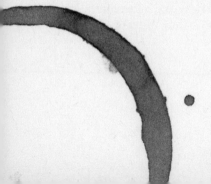

BLACK BUTTER

Black Butter, *Du Nier Beurre*, is a traditional preserve from Jersey, in the Channel Islands, made in vast quantities every November with the island's apple crop. Local women would get together to peel hundred of pounds of apples, and the fire would be lit in the afternoon and cooking would go on through the night and well into the next day. This is the traditional recipe: you may want to reduce the quantities.

> 38l (10 gallons) cider
> 318 kg (700 lb) sweet apples, peeled and cut
> 9 kg (20 lb) sugar
> 3 sticks liquorice, finely chopped
> 24 lemons, sliced
> 3 lb allspice

Boil the cider in a bachin (a huge cauldron) until it turns to jelly. Add the apples, stirring constantly to prevent sticking. Two hours after the last batch of apples has been stirred in, add the sugar, liquorice and lemons. Stir constantly for 30 hours (yes, 30), adding the spice in the last ten minutes. Store in jars and use in desserts such as bread and butter pudding, crumbles and ice cream, or served on toast, crumpets and scones.

VODKA

There cannot be not enough snacks,
There can only be not enough vodka.
There can be no silly jokes,
There can only be not enough vodka.
There can be no ugly women,
There can only be not enough vodka.
There cannot be too much vodka,
There can only be not enough vodka.
Russian proverb

PEPPER VODKA CHICKEN

Pertsovka is the Russian name for pepper vodka. Vodka itself means 'little water' – not so little in sufficient quantities. This dish has a good kick – you can replicate it with regular vodka and a good couple of teaspoonfuls of Tabasco.

1 whole chicken
salt & fresh ground pepper
2 tbsp olive oil
1 small onion, finely chopped
1 small carrot, peeled and sliced into 1/4" coins
1 bunch fresh thyme
80ml (1/3 cup) pepper vodka

Preheat the oven 230C/450F/Gas Mark 8. Cut the chicken into pieces: thighs, drumsticks, wings and halved breasts. Season with salt and pepper, and cook in the olive oil for a few minutes in a large pot over a medium-high heat. When nicely brown, pour the vodka over and light. When this burns, add the onion, carrot and thyme, stir, and place in the oven.

Roast for 30-45 minutes until the chicken is fully cooked.

PENNE ALLA VODKA

This is a classic recipe, a good solid dish with a whiff of booze. Makes enough sauce for two – use as much pasta (preferably penne, but any will do) as you like.

> 1 tin chopped tomatoes
> 2 cloves garlic, crushed
> 2 shallots, finely chopped
> 1 tbsp olive oil
> 1 tbsp butter
> 250ml (1 cup) stock
> 125ml (1/2 cup) double cream
> big handful of fresh basil, chopped
> 250ml (1 cup) vodka

Melt the butter in a large pan, add the oil, garlic and shallots and sauté for a few minutes to soften. Add the vodka and allow to reduce for a couple of minutes, then add the stock and the tomatoes, bring to the boil, then allow to simmer.

Meanwhile, cook the pasta and drain. When ready, stir the cream into the sauce, bring to the boil again, then remove from the heat. Toss the warm pasta in the sauce and basil leaves and serve.

MEATBALLS IN VODKA SAUCE

A hearty dish, for 8-12 people, and worth making in quantity.

For the sauce:
1 tbsp olive oil
1 small onion, finely chopped
4 cloves garlic, crushed
2 tins chopped tomatoes
1 small tin tomato paste
1 large carrot, finely chopped
2 tbsp fresh oregano, finely chopped (or 2 tsp dried)
500ml (2 cups) water
75ml (1/4 cup) vodka

For the meatballs:
700g (1 1/2 lbs) ground beef
225g (1/2 lb) Italian-style pork sausage, well chopped
2 large eggs, slightly beaten
55g (2 oz) bread crumbs
3 cloves garlic, crushed
1 small onion, finely chopped
1 tbsp fresh oregano, finely chopped (or 1 tsp dried)
24 small balls fresh mozzarella cheese

To make the sauce, heat the oil in a pan and sauté the onions until soft, then add the garlic and cook for another minute. Add the tinned tomatoes and tomato paste, and the carrots, oregano, water and vodka, stirring gently. Simmer gently until the sauce thickens and the vegetable are all soft. Add extra water if it gets too thick. Season to taste.

While the sauce is cooking, preheat the oven to 200C/400F/Gas Mark 6. Mix the ground beef, sausage, eggs, bread crumbs, garlic, onion, oregano and some salt and pepper in a bowl. For each meatball, take two tablespoons of the mixture and press a small mozzarella ball into the center, rolling the meat completely around it. Repeat until you've used all the meat.

Bake the meatballs in the oven for about 25 minutes, checking they're cooked all the way through. When done, put them in with the sauce, and serve with hot pasta.

VODKA MARTINI SMOKED SALMON

A classy barbecue dish this is – quite a step up from Beer Butt Chicken. Use good wood chips for flavour, and make sure you leave plenty of time to cook it right though.

> 1 1.3 - 1.8kg (3-4 lb) salmon, cleaned
> 6 sprigs fresh dill
> 60ml (1/4 cup) lemon juice
> 3 tbsp butter, melted
> 1 tbsp horseradish
> 2 cloves garlic, crushed
> 1 lemon, sliced
> 1/2 tsp tabasco
> 60ml (1/4 cup) vodka
> 60ml (1/4 cup) vermouth

Wash the salmon and dry well. Fill with dill and lemon slices and set it aside. Place the butter, lemon juice, horseradish, garlic, tabasco and booze in a small saucepan and bring to the boil. Remove and allow to cool. Wrap the salmon in a large piece of foil, leaving one side open. Pour in the sauce, and close loosely. Place on the edge of the grill for about an hour, to cook gently. After an hour, open one side of the package, and cook for another hour. Check it's properly cooked before slicing and serving.

STRAWBERRIES ROMANOFF

Strawberries Romanoff, in this version, originate with the great French pasty chef Marie Antoine Careme (1784-1833), who cooked for the Russian Tsar Nicholas I. Careme was the author of one of the first great cookbooks, the 5-volume *L'Art de la Cuisine Française*, as well as working as personal chef to such figures as the French statesman Talleyrand, the Baron Rothschild, and the Prince Regent, later King George IV.

> *4 cups fresh strawberries*
> *55g (2 oz) icing sugar*
> *125ml (1/4 pint) vodka*
> *125ml (1/4 pint) triple sec*
> *125ml (1/4 pint) rum*
>
> *For the cream:*
> *250g (9 oz) plus 3 tbsp cream*
> *55g (2 oz) sugar*
> *1 tsp gelatin*
> *250ml (1/2 pint) sour cream*
> *1/2 tsp vanilla*

Wash and hull the strawberries and toss in the sugar. Place in a large bowl and pour in vodka, triple sec and rum. For the Russian cream, mix the cream, sugar and gelatin in a saucepan and heat gently until the gelatin is dissolved. Cool and allow to thicken slightly, then fold in the sour cream and vanilla. Whisk until smooth and pour into a small bowl or mould.

To serve, invert the mould onto a plate and surround with piles of the soaked strawberries.

MARINATED PLUMS

"I have a punishing workout regimen. Every day I do 3 minutes on a treadmill, then I lie down, drink a glass of vodka and smoke a cigarette."—Anthony Hopkins

> 2 plums, sliced
> 1 tbsp sugar
> 1/2 tbsp grated lemon peel
> lemon sorbet
> 75ml (1/4 cup) chilled vodka

Mix plums, sugar, lemon and vodka in a bowl, stirring until the sugar dissolves. Chill in the fridge for at least an hour to let the juice soak. Spoon over the sorbet to serve. Makes enough for 2.

HARVEY WALLBANGER CAKE

All of the people who've ever looked at the drink in their hand and thought "Hey, this is great and all, but what would make it really special is if it was a *cake*,"—this one's for you. To make it easier we've used ready-made cake mix, but feel free to bake from scratch.

> 500g (18 oz) yellow cake mix
> 350g (13 oz) vanilla instant pudding mix
> 1 cup oil
> 4 eggs
> 200ml (3/4) cup orange juice
> 75ml (1/4 cup) Galliano liqueur
> 75ml (1/4 cup) vodka
>
> For the glaze:
> 130g (4 1/2 oz) sifted icing sugar
> 1 tbsp orange juice
> 1 tbsp Galliano
> 1 tsp vodka

Preheat the oven to 180C/350F/Gas Mark 4. Mix all the ingredients together (preferably in a mixer at medium speed) for several minutes. Grease and flour a cake tin, either a bundt (doughnut-shaped tin) or a round one, and pour the mix into it. Bake for 45-50 minutes.

For the glaze, mix the icing sugar, remaining orange juice, Galliano and vodka, and spoon this over the warm cake.

WATERMELON VODKA

There are recipes in this book that require a lot of work, taste delicious, but yield rather less in terms of alcoholic effect than might be hoped for. There are others which require little work, taste delicious, and have the potential to get you hammered. This is one of the latter.

> 1 *large watermelon*
> 1 *bottle vodka*

Cut a hole in one end of the watermelon large enough to admit a funnel. Keep upright in the fridge (if it will fit), and over several days, pour in the vodka until the watermelon is saturated. Eat.

VODKA JELLY

Vodka jellies have a fearsome reputation, usually because of bizarrely high levels of spirit. While your tolerance and hangover levels are entirely up to you, exhaustive research suggests that you're best sticking with the manufacturer's proportions, to make sure the jelly sets correctly. If in doubt, make more jellies, not stronger ones.

> *jelly cubes (orange and lime flavours are best, but it's a matter of taste)*
> *water*
> *vodka*

Most manufacturers suggest melting their product in a certain amount of boiling water, then adding an equal amount of cold water. Instead of cold water, simply use chilled vodka, then allow to set (small bowls and glasses are good if you don't have moulds).

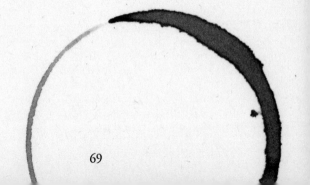

WHISKY

"The water was not fit to drink. To make it palatable, we had to add whisky. By diligent effort, I learnt to like it."
Winston Churchill

COLLOPS OF VENISON

Scotch collops are an ancient dish, which can be made with beef, lamb or venison. This is the latter, and it's bloody lovely. Serves 4.

> 4 180g (6 oz) venison steaks (or sirloin steaks)
> 30g (1 oz) butter
> 2 small apples, cored and sliced
> 1 tsp honey
> 250g (9 oz) double cream
> 5 juniper berries, crushed
> parsley, to garnish
> 2 tbsp whisky

Melt the butter in a large frying pan and cook the steaks. Place in the oven to keep them warm while you make the sauce. Fry the apple slices until hot, then mix the whisky, honey, cream and berries together and add them to the pan. When sauce is hot, pour over the steaks, garnish with parsley, and serve.

WHISKY STEAK

Nothing better than a hearty steak to warm the cockles, so the addition of a good shot of whisky makes it all the better. This recipe is for one – vary the quantities according to how hungry you are.

sirloin steak
25g (1 oz) butter
1 medium onion, chopped
125g (5 oz) double cream
salt and pepper
5 tbsp whisky

Heat the butter in a pan, cut the beef into thin strips and cook it with the onion for 5-10 minutes, until brown and to your taste. Pour the whisky over it, and stir in the cream. Allow the sauce to reduce a little before serving.

MUSHROOM AND WHISKY SOUP

Whisky gives this mushroom soup the little kick it needs to make it really interesting. Why not, eh? Serves 2, or 1 hungry.

350g (1 lb) mushrooms, sliced
2 large onions, chopped
1 tbsp French mustard
1 litre (2 pints) stock
150g (5 oz) ham, finely chopped
375ml (12 oz) powdered milk
2 tbsp whisky

Cook the mushrooms and onions in the stock and mustard, simmering gently. After 20 minutes, add the ham, powdered milk and whisky and heat through, being careful not to boil. Serve with lots of brown bread and butter.

WHISKY SCALLOPS

The delicate taste of scallops is much improved by a robust whisky sauce. Serves 6.

> 24 scallops
> 3 tbsp cream (or crème fraîche)
> 2 tbsp olive oil
> 6 leeks
> 3 tbsp whisky

Wash the leeks well and slice into thin discs. Fry gently in a pan for 10 minutes, until soft. Set them aside. Heat the oil in the pan and cook the scallops for two minutes at a time (in batches if necessary – make sure each is cooked properly). Set them aside also. Pour the whisky into the pan and warm, then remove from the heat and stir in the cream. Season with salt and pepper to taste. Arrange the scallops and leeks on a plate and drizzle with the sauce.

WHISKY MARINATED SALMON

Scotland. Where the lasses are bonnie, the men wear skirts, and even the fish drink whisky. You take the high road, I'll take the low road, and so on.

225g (8 oz) boned fillet of salmon
2 tbsp lemon juice
1/2 tsp sugar
salt and pepper
1 tsp chopped chives
1 tbsp chopped dill
2 tbsp whisky

Place the salmon in the freezer for at least an hour before starting. Using a very sharp knife slice the fish as finely as possible across the grain. Lay the slices on top of each other on a high-sided dish. Pour the lemon juice and whisky all over the pile and season with salt and pepper. Sprinkle with the sugar and then the herbs. Best left overnight to marinate, although a couple of hours will do, and give it a good rub with the juices before serving.

Chicken in Apple and Whisky Sauce

"I just had 19 shots of whiskey, I think that's a record."—Dylan Thomas's last words.

4 chicken breasts
15g (1/2 oz) butter
2 apples, peeled and sliced
zest of 1 lemon
freshly ground black pepper
1 tbsp chopped fresh tarragon
15g (1/2 oz) plain flour
125ml (1/4 pint) chicken stock
125ml (1/4 pint) cup milk
3 tbsp whipping cream
75ml whisky

Melt the butter in a pan and sauté the chicken, turning regularly. After 10 minutes, add the apples, lemon zest, pepper and tarragon and cook for a further 15 minutes until the apple softens and the chicken is fully cooked. Stir in the flour and cook for 1 minute, slowly adding the stock and milk and allowing the sauce to thicken, then boil. Stir in the cream and the whisky and heat through before serving.

WILD TURKEY WILD TURKEY

"How well I remember my first encounter with The Devil's Brew. I happened to stumble across a case of bourbon – and went right on stumbling for several days thereafter."
—W.C. Fields

> 1 wild turkey breast (although farmed will do, I
>   suppose)
> 125ml (1/2 cup) honey
> 2 tbsp Worcestershire sauce
> 3 tbsp Dijon mustard
> 1 tbsp plain flour
> 1 tsp cajun pepper or other hot sauce
> oil for frying
> 225g (8 oz) grated cheddar cheese
> 1/2 cup chopped onion
> 500ml (1/2 pint) Wild Turkey bourbon

Cut the turkey into 5cm (2 inch) strips, removing the skin. Heat the honey to loosen it up and mix in the Worcestershire sauce, mustard and bourbon to make the marinade. Marinate the turkey in the fridge for at least a couple of hours.

Mix the flour and seasoning in a bag, and shake the turkey strips in it to coat them, then fry in the oil until browned and cooked through. Sprinkle with the cheese and onion and place beneath a hot grill to melt the cheese, then serve with rice, or alone.

WHISKY GLAZED MUSHROOMS

"Always carry a large flagon of whisky in case of snakebite and furthermore always carry a small snake."
—W.C. Fields

170g (6 oz) sliced shiitake mushrooms
2 tbsp olive oil
1 clove garlic, finely chopped
2 shallots, finely chopped
1/2 tbsp ginger, crushed
1/2 tsp juniper berries, crushed
150ml (1/4 pint) stock
1 tbsp fresh lemon juice.
1 tbsp dark brown sugar
150ml (1/4 pint) whisky

Mix the whisky and the brown sugar in a bowl. Heat 1 tbsp oil in a frying pan and when hot add the mushrooms and sauté, adding more oil as needed, until the mushrooms start to release their liquid. Add the garlic, shallots, ginger and juniper, stirring quickly, and cook for two minutes, taking care not to burn and turning the heat down if necessary. Add the whisky and sugar mixture and light. When burned out, turn up the heat and add the stock, boiling hard for about three minutes until the mushrooms are glazed. Season with the lemon juice and salt and pepper.

HIGHLAND FONDUE

"Freedom and Whisky gang thegither!"—Robert Burns

> 1 small onion, finely chopped
> 3 tsp butter
> 250ml (1/2 pt) milk
> 450g (1 lb) Scottish or mature cheddar cheese, grated
> 3 tsp cornflour
> 4 tbsp Scotch whisky

Cook the onion in the butter in a large pan for a few minutes until soft. Add milk and continue heating until the milk starts to bubble. Gradually stir in the cheese and cook until all is melted, stirring continuously. In a small bowl, mix the whisky and cornflour, then add to the cheese. Cook for a further couple of minutes to thicken then transfer to a serving pot. Serve with plenty of cubes of onion bread for dipping.

WHISKY RAREBIT

If you're going to do something, do it well. This is much more than your average cheese on toast.

> 28g (1 oz) butter
> 170g (6 oz) cheddar cheese, grated
> dash of English mustard
> 1 egg yolk
> 1 egg white, stiffly beaten
> 1 tbsp whisky

Melt the butter in a pan and add the grated cheese, whisky, mustard and some salt and pepper. Stir over a very low heat until the mixture melts smooth. Remove from the heat and stir in the egg yolk, then fold in the white with a metal spoon. Spoon over four slices of hot toast and place beneath a medium grill. Ready when brown and bubbling.

TIPSY SWEET POTATOES

This Southern US dish is best made with bourbon, in honour of its heritage. Serves 6-8 as a side dish.

> *450g (1 lb) sweet potatoes*
> *4 tbsp butter, softened*
> *55g (2 oz) light brown sugar*
> *pinch of salt*
> *pecan halves or marshmallow for topping*
> *125ml (1/4 pint) bourbon whiskey*

Preheat the over to 160C/325F/Gas Mark 3. Cook the potatoes for about 15 minutes or until they are soft and slide off a knife. Drain, mash and add the butter, sugar, salt and whiskey. Spoon the mixture into a casserole dish and sprinkle with the topping of choice. Bake in the oven for 20 to 25 minutes until piping hot and bubbly.

SWEET ORANGE SINGLE MALT DRESSING

Unlike most of the other recipes in this chapter, where the cooking will destroy most of the unique character of a whisky so blends are fine, we recommend a single malt for this one because you'll really taste it. A good unpeated lowland malt is best.

2 tbsp orange juice
1 tbsp honey
2 tsp dried thyme
2 tbsp balsamic vinegar
100ml (1/3 cup) extra virgin olive oil
pinch salt
1 tbsp whisky

Whisk all the ingredients together – preferably several hours before the meal – and allow to sit for a while. Excellent with strong, peppery or goats' cheese salads.

WHISKY AND HONEY CAKE

An ancient Scotch relative taught me this recipe when I was but a wee slip of a lad. The sort of thing to sit down to after tossing a few cabers and killing a few Englishmen. With a nice cup of tea.

> *170g (6 oz) self-raising flour*
> *170g (6 oz) butter*
> *170g (6 oz) soft brown sugar*
> *3 eggs, beaten*
> *Rind of a small orange, grated*
> *4 tbsp whisky*
>
> *For the icing:*
> *170g (6 oz) icing sugar*
> *55g (2 oz) butter*
> *2 tbsp honey*
> *Juice from a small orange*
> *110g (3 oz) toasted almond flakes*

Preheat the over to 190C/375F/Gas Mark 5. Mix the butter and sugar together well, add the orange rind and beat in the eggs one at a time. Whisk until the mixture is pale and fluffy. Sift in half the flour and add the whisky. Fold into the mixture, and then sift in the remaining flour. Grease two round cake tins and divide the mixture between them, spreading it evenly. Bake in the oven for 20-25 minutes until a light golden colour. Cool on a rack.

For the icing, mix the butter, honey, and a tbsp of orange juice in a mixing bowl. Slowly sift in the icing sugar and stir until they are well mixed. Use half the cream as filling between the two halves of the cake and spread the rest on the top, sprinkling the almonds over it.

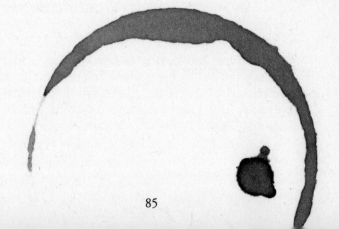

WHISKY PANCAKES

You can do a lot of good things with these pancakes. I like to eat them with raspberries and cream, or coated in melted chocolate, but your own favourite way is best. Makes 4.

> *55g (2 oz) plain flour*
> *pinch of salt*
> *1 egg*
> *150ml (1/4 pint) milk*
> *2 tsp groundnut or other flavourless oil*
> *300ml (1/2 pint) orange juice*
> *2 tbsp honey*
> *15g (1/2 oz) butter*
> *3 tbsp whisky*

Sift the flour and the salt into a large bowl. Make a hole in the centre and break the egg into it. Gradually whisk in the milk to form a smooth batter. Heat a frying pan, pour in the oil and then wipe it clean with kitchen paper. Pour just enough batter in to coat the base and cook for about a minute. Give it a shake to loosen it up, then toss and cook the other side. Repeat with the rest of the batter, then put the pancakes aside.

Pour the orange juice into the frying pan and add the honey and butter. Bring to the boil and simmer for 5 minutes to reduce the sauce, then pour in the whisky. Fold the pancakes into quarters and place them in the simmering sauce for 30 seconds to warm though.

WHISKY AND ORANGE MOUSSE

"Too much of anything is bad, but too much of good whiskey is barely enough."—Mark Twain

170g (6 oz) dark chocolate
5 tbsp water
3 eggs
2 egg yolks
55g (2 oz) fine caster sugar
1 tsp gelatin
juice from one orange
250ml (1/2 pint) double cream
2 tbsp whisky

Heat the water in a small pan and melt the chocolate, stirring until creamy. Beat the egg, egg yolks and sugar together in a bowl until thick and pale. Put the orange juice in another bowl in a pan of warm water and dissolve the gelatin into it, before stirring in the whisky. Fold the melted chocolate and egg mixtures together then stir in the gelatin mixture. Whip the cream until it starts to thicken, then fold that in too. Spoon into glasses or small bowls and put them into the fridge to chill.

MEXICAN WHISKY CANDY

Those crazy Mexicans. This makes a nice bagful.

> 110g (4 oz) brown sugar
> 130g (4 1/2 oz) white sugar
> 125ml (1/4 pint) sour cream
> 200g (3 1/2 oz) pecans, shelled and halved
> 1 tsp vanilla
> 2 tbsp whisky (preferably bourbon)

Mix the sugar and sour cream and cook slowly over a low heat until it forms a soft ball. Remove from the heat and mix in the vanilla, nuts and the bourbon. Stir well until thick and creamy. With a spoon, drip lumps onto wax paper and allow to cool.

IRISH WHISKEY SODA BREAD

I'm more of a Scotch man myself, but there's no doubt the Irish know a thing or two about the drink. Of course, you can make this with either, but it's good to follow the old ways.

100g (3 1/2 oz) raisins
4 tbsp butter, softened
150g (5 oz) plain flour
150g (5 oz) whole wheat flour
3 tbsp sugar
1 tsp baking soda
3/4 tsp salt
180ml (1/3 pint) buttermilk
250ml (1/2 pint) Irish whiskey

Preheat oven to 190C/375F/Gas Mark 5. Soak the raisins in the whiskey for at least half an hour, then drain and save the whiskey. In a large bowl, stir together the flour, sugar, baking soda and salt. Rub the butter into the mixture with your fingers until it resembles coarse crumbs, then stir in the raisins. With a wooden spoon, stir in buttermilk until the mixture moistens and sticks together. Knead the dough until smooth but still a bit sticky, then pat into a round about 15cm (6 inches) across and 5cm (2 inches) high. Score a deep cross into the top of the loaf, 1cm (1/2 inch) deep then bake on the middle shelf for 30 minutes. Best served warm.

IRISH WHISKEY BUTTER

This is pretty much perfect with Irish whiskey soda bread.
And Irish whiskey.

> *1 tbsp sugar*
> *9 tbsp butter, softened*
> *3 tbsp whiskey*

Heat the whiskey and sugar in a pan until hot then stir
in the butter until melted and fully combined. Allow
to cool.

CHOCOLATE WHISKY BALLS

Using crumbled cookies makes these fantastically rich and chocolatey. Vary whisky strength according to taste...

110g (4 oz) pecans, finely chopped
175g (6 oz) chocolate cookies
130g (4 1/2 oz) icing sugar
icing sugar for rolling
1 1/2 tbsp golden syrup or corn syrup
125ml (1/2 cup) whisky

Crumble the chocolate cookies as finely as possible, and mix with the nuts in a large bowl. Add the sugar, syrup and whisky, mixing thoroughly with your hands. Roll the mixture into balls and roll in the icing sugar. Place in the fridge in a sealed container, or freeze on a tray and place in sealed bags.

DOM PEDRO

The legendary Dom Pedro is served a number of ways, often blended and served in a glass as a cocktail, or here as a dessert. Nuts optional.

>*2 scoops vanilla ice cream*
>*chocolate sauce*
>*2 shots single malt whisky*

Drizzle chocolate sauce over the ice cream and give it a good stir to start the ice cream melting, then pour over the whisky.

PEACHES IN WHISKY

"I like my whisky old and my women young."—Errol Flynn

> 8 ripe peaches, peeled and halved
> 900g (2 lb) very fine sugar
> 300ml (2/3 pint) water
> 250g (9 oz) whipped cream
> 3 tbsp whisky

Heat the water, dissolving in the sugar as you bring it to the boil. Add the peaches and simmer for 15 minutes. Remove the peaches and add the whisky to the syrup, boiling for five minutes. Cool and pour over the peaches. Chill and serve with whipped cream.

RUM

"There's naught, no doubt, so much the spirit calms
as rum and true religion"
Lord Byron

RUM RABBIT TERRINE

This is an astonishingly rich dish, which requires quite a lot of preparation, but is absolutely worth it for the gamey flavours backed by the dark sweetness of the rum.

> *1 rabbit*
> *5-6 chicken livers, cubed*
> *900g (2 lb) loin or leg of pork*
> *1 clove garlic, crushed*
> *450g (1 lb) extra pork fat*
> *1 tsp ground ginger*
> *55g (2 oz) pistachios, split*
> *1 beaten egg*
> *340g (12 oz) streaky bacon*
> *3 tbsps Jamaican Rum*
> *8 fl oz rosé or dry white wine*

Bone the rabbit, separating the two back fillets. Cut the back fillets into 2cm (1/2 inch) cubes and place in a sealed container with the cubed chicken livers and marinade overnight in the rum. At the same time, put the pork meat and remaining rabbit meat to marinate overnight in the wine with the garlic.

Next day, preheat the over to 180C/350F/Gas Mark 4 and mince the wine-marinated meat with the pork fat using the fine blade of a mincer. Mix in the wine from the marinade, the ginger, drained fillet and chicken livers, and the pistachio nuts. Add the rum, juices and beaten egg. Season well with salt and pepper. Line a terrine or seamless loaf tin with the bacon and pack in the mixture.

Cover with buttered foil. Stand this in a second container of hot water (a bain-marie) and bake in the oven for 1 1/2 - 1 3/4 hours.

Remove the foil half an hour before the end of the cooking time. A terrine is cooked when the juices run quite clear. Cool before pressing it with a board and 3-4lb scale weights or an equivalent load, and refrigerate. Serve cut into elegant slices with a watercress salad and fingers of lemon-buttered brown toast.

RUM COFFEE RISOTTO

Don't be afraid of this recipe – it's quite special. Instant coffee is actually an excellent ingredient in dishes, particularly in one's more impecunious times – and when poor, what else would one be buying but booze? Serves 2-4.

> 2 tbsp instant coffee granules
> zest and juice of one orange
> 150g (5 oz) arborio rice
> 1 litre (2 pints) milk
> 2 drops vanilla extract
> 150g (5 oz) sugar
> 4 tbsp butter
> 300g (10 oz) double cream
> 6 tbsp rum

Mix the coffee granules and orange juice in a saucepan with 125ml (1/2 cup) of water and bring to the boil. Immediately remove from the heat and stir in the rice. Soak for 5 minutes then return to the heat and stir in the milk and vanilla extract. Cook over a low heat, stirring constantly, until the rice is tender but *al dente*. Remove from the heat, stir in the orange zest, butter, cream, sugar and rum, and serve.

Chocolate Rum Fondue

The traditional cheese fondue has always been a boozy dish, ever since its invention by the Swiss centuries ago – the first recorded admixture with wine occurred in Zurich in 1699. This rather more modern version continues the tradition – best served with chunks of fruit, for the grown-up, and marshmallows, for the less so.

> *200g (7 oz) milk chocolate, broken up*
> *2 tbsp butter*
> *2 tbsp plain yoghurt*
> *150g (5 oz) double cream*
> *2 tbsp white rum*
> *dips of choice*

Heat the butter, yoghurt and cream over a low heat, stirring constantly until well mixed and hot – but don't allow to boil. Stir in the rum then remove from the heat and add the chocolate, whisking until smooth. Pour into fondue pot and serve.

Banana Flambé

Although the practice of igniting food for show can be traced to the Moors in the 14th century, modern flambéing was discovered in Monte Carlo in 1895, when Henri Carpentier, a waiter, accidentally set fire to a pan of crêpes he was preparing for the future Edward VII – and found the dish much improved.

> 2 bananas
> 2 tbsp sunflower oil
> 4 tbsp sugar
> juice of one lime
> 125ml (1/4 pint) white rum

Peel the bananas and cut them in half lengthwise. Heat the oil in a medium pan and brown the bananas for 5 minutes on each side. Add the sugar and the rum and cook for a couple of minutes then light. When the flames go out, sprinkle with lime juice and serve.

RUM OMELETTE

This is a pudding omelette, a rare thing these days, courtesy of the late, great Mrs Beeton. But who says you have to have it for pudding? A fine meal, then, at any time.

> *3 eggs*
> *1 tbsp caster sugar*
> *1 tbsp cream*
> *1 tbsp butter*
> *2 tbsp rum*

Beat the eggs well and stir in the sugar, cream and half the rum. Heat the butter over a hot heat and pour in the eggs as soon as it starts to foam. Keep stirring until the eggs start to set, then start folding, cooking for a further minute or so, then tip out onto a hot dish. Pour the rest of the rum over and ignite. Extinguish before eating.

You can of course use almost any liqueur for this although obviously the more flammable ones are more rewarding.

RUM PIE

Nanny used to make this for special occasions. Fine filly, nanny, although she used to scald her udders terribly on the element. Watch you don't do the same.

> *short pastry*
> *250ml (1/2 pint) milk, with a pinch of nutmeg*
> *55g (2 oz) sugar*
> *2 eggs*
> *1 1/2 tsp gelatine*
> *1 tsp cornflour*
> *2 tbsp rum, plus a little extra*
>
> *For the topping:*
> *2 tbsp cream*
> *1 tsp sugar*
> *55g (2 oz) chocolate*
> *2 tbsp water*

Bake the pastry in a shallow dish. Beat the egg yolks with sugar and a pinch of salt until thick, then stir in the cornflour and heat the milk, gradually adding it to the mixture. Heat the lot gently, then stir in the gelatine (dissolved in a little water) and allow to cool. Then fold in the beaten egg whites and add the rum. When cooled, pour into the pastry case.

Melt the chocolate in the water over a gentle heat, then while it's cooling, whip the cream with the sugar and a dash more rum, before mixing both together. Cover the pie with the result and chill the lot to serve.

Mojito Cupcakes

There's plenty of debate about the origins of the Mojito. While most claim it was invented some time in the 1800s, others trace it back to much earlier – to the 1500s – and a concoction known as *El Draque*. *El Draque* was allegedly created by English pirate Richard Drake in honour of his boss, Sir Francis Drake, with *aguardiente* (fire water), a precursor to rum. Mull it over while you munch on some of these (makes 12).

80g (3 oz) sugar
200g (7 oz) flour
1/4 tsp salt
2 tsp baking powder
zest and juice of half a lime
handful of fresh mint, finely chopped
50g (2 oz) butter, melted
1 egg
250ml (1 cup) milk
1 shot dark rum

For the icing:
110g (4 oz) butter
1 tbsp milk
200g (7 oz) icing sugar

Preheat the oven to 180C/350F/Gas Mark 4. Mix the sugar, flour, salt and baking powder in a large bowl. In a smaller bowl, beat the egg with the melted butter, then gently whisk that into the larger bowl, then stir in the milk and rum until smooth. Add half the zest and lime juice, then the mint, stirring all the time. Divide the batter evenly between 12 paper cupcake wrappers and bake for 10-12 minutes, until golden and spongy. Place on a rack and cool.

For the icing, beat the butter and the icing sugar very hard in a bowl until fluffy. Add the milk, the remaining lime juice and zest, and beat some more. Spread over the cooled cupcakes, and consume.

BRANDY

"Claret is the liquor for boys; port for men; but he who aspires to be a hero must drink brandy."
Samuel Johnson

BRANDY BUTTER

Brandy Butter is traditionally served with Christmas puddings, but its all-you-can-drink ethos shouldn't be ignored at other times of the year. It goes just as well with hot puddings such as crumbles and pies.

> *110g (4 oz) unsalted butter*
> *110g (4 oz) caster sugar (or half icing / half caster)*
> *As much brandy as you can beat into it (4-6*
> *tablespoons)*

Beat butter and sugar together until the mixture whitens – this is called creaming. Add a spoonful of brandy at a time, beating it in each time, until it will not take any more. Chill in the fridge, where it will keep for up to a week.

FINEST BRANDY GRAVY

If you can't wait until the end of the meal for a stiff drink, better pour it over the main course. This recipe doesn't muck about: it's proper gravy made with demi-glace, and excellent with any roast meat – although turkey is a particular favourite.

45g (1 1/2 oz) pot veal or chicken demi-glace
1 tablespoon unsalted butter
125ml (1/2 cup) double cream
125ml (1/2 cup) water
1 tablespoon brandy
freshly ground pepper

Put the brandy, water and demi-glace in a small pan over a medium-high heat. Bring it slowly to the boil, stirring all the time until smooth. Stir in the butter and turn the heat down, and keep stirring until the gravy thickens after about a minute. Stir in the cream, season to taste with pepper, and serve nice and hot.

BRANDY WAFERS

What better symbol of the Auld Alliance than these traditional Scotch wafers with a good dose of French brandy? Well, apart from a fine malt matured in cognac barrels. But enough of that; give these a try in your ice cream.

> 50g (2 oz) golden syrup
> 50g (2 oz) butter
> 50g (2 oz) 2 oz plain flour
> 50g (2 oz) 2 oz castor sugar
> 1/2 tsp ground ginger
> 1 tsp brandy

Preheat the oven to 250C/450F/Gas Mark 8 and grease a baking sheet. Melt the butter, syrup and sugar over a gentle heat and then stir in the flour, ginger and brandy. Keep stirring for about five minutes. Drop small teaspoonfuls onto the baking sheet, keeping them well apart. Bake for five minutes or until they are a pale golden brown. While they're still hot, wrap them round the greased handle of a wooden spoon to form spirals, then allow to cool.

Mushrooms a le Carré

I call them that because they make me all Smiley. Sorry.
Serves 2 – or one hungry spy.

350g (12 oz) mushrooms, washed and chopped
2 tbsp butter
1 clove garlic, chopped
1 very small onion, chopped
fresh lemon juice
salt and pepper
285ml (1/2 pint) double cream
chopped fresh chervil
3 tbsp brandy

Melt the butter in a heavy pan and gently fry the onion
and garlic for a few minutes. Add the mushrooms
and a little lemon juice. Cook gently until all the liquid
has evaporated, then add the brandy and cream and cook
gently until the mixture has thickened. Season to taste
and serve on toast and garnished with chervil.

BRANDY BAKED BRIE

Go on, say it. Say "Wheel of Cheese". Sounds good, doesn't it?

> 375ml (1 1/2 cup) brown sugar
> 225g (1/2 lb) walnuts, finely chopped
> 1 (900g/2 lb) wheel of brie
> 125ml (1/2 cup) brandy

In a small bowl, mix the brown sugar, brandy and walnuts. Place brie on top of something you can put in the oven (a small grill pan will do) and spoon the walnut mixture over top, covering it completely. Wrap the brie and pan in clingfilm and stick it in the fridge for a good couple of hours. When ready, preheat the oven to 205C (400F), unwrap the brie and bake for 10 to 15 minutes – until it starts to melt. Allow to cool a little before serving with thin toast or crackers.

BRANDY CUSTARD

A good alternative to brandy butter, this – and an absolute godsend for the aged relative's Christmas Cake. But don't feel you need to save it for the festive season.

> 1 vanilla pod, halved lengthways
> 2 cups double cream
> 275ml (1/2 pint) milk
> 9 egg yolks
> 1/2 cup castor sugar
> 3 tsp cornflour
> 2 tbsp brandy

Scrape the seeds out of the vanilla pod, and put the lot into a saucepan with the cream and milk. Cook over a very low heat for 20 minutes or so until hot (don't let it boil), then put it aside for twenty minutes and strain out the vanilla bits. In a large bowl, beat the egg yolks, sugar and cornflour hard until think and pale, then add the vanilla cream, stirring constantly. Pour the mixture into the pan and cook, stirring constantly, over a medium-low heat for 20 minutes – until the custard thickens and coats the back of a metal spoon. Pour in the brandy and cook for a couple minutes more to let it infuse. Serve warm.

HUNGARIAN BRANDY BEEF GOULASH

Fine camp cooks, the Magyars. Used to boil this up on the hoof when marauding. Has much the same effect today – don't be afraid to add plenty of paprika for that "I fancy another crack at the Ottomans" feeling.

> 1 kg (2 lb) stewing beef, cut into 2.5cm (1") cubes
> 4 large onions (about 1 kg/2 lb), chopped
> 2 tbsp paprika
> 1 tin chopped tomatoes
> 3 tbsp cooking oil
> 2 tsp salt
> 1 tsp pepper
> 3/4 tsp marjoram, crumbled
> 3/4 tsp caraway seeds
> 1 tsp cornflour
> 500ml stock
> 200ml brandy

Toss the beef with the salt, pepper and paprika until coated. Heat the oil in a large pan and brown the meat, then add the onions and cook for 5 minutes. Remove from the heat, pour half the brandy over, and ignite (do be careful). When the flames die out, stick it back on the heat and add the stock. Cover tightly and simmer for an hour or so, until the meat is tender. Add the marjoram and caraway, and mix in the cornflour and remaining brandy. Stir until the sauce thickens, then tuck in.

WALNUT AND BRANDY CAKE

The English were so appalled by the arrival of the *nux Gallica* from the continent they named it *wealhhnutu*, or 'foreign nut'. Luckily, we've come round to it since then.

> *250g (8 oz) 70% chocolate*
> *350g (12 oz) butter*
> *300g (10 oz) shelled walnuts, blended, or chopped as*
> *fine as possible*
> *4 eggs*
> *220g (7 oz) caster sugar*
> *3 tbsps brandy*

Preheat the oven to 160/Gas Mark 3. Melt the chocolate and butter in a dish over a pan of hot water. Beat the sugar and the egg yolks together, and add them slowly to the chocolate, stirring constantly, then fold in the walnuts. Then beat in the egg whites until the mixture starts to solidify and pour the lot into a greased and lined, 25cm cake tin.

Bake in the oven for 10 minutes. Reduce the heat to 150/ Gas 2 and continue baking for another 45 minutes, then allow to cool. When done, turn out of the tin, and pour the brandy all over it. Mmmm.

TEQUILA

"When life hands you lemons –
break out the tequila and salt"
George Carlin

Grilled Margarita Wings

There are many claimants to the title of creator of the Margarita, but one of the strongest is Daniel Negrete. The Negrete family story goes that Daniel opened a bar at the Garci Crispo hotel in Puebla, Mexico, with his brother, David. The day before David's marriage in 1936, Daniel presented the original cocktail as a wedding present to Margarita, his sister-in-law.

> *900g (2 lbs) chicken wings, cut into 2 pieces at the joint*
> *65ml (1/4 cup) frozen orange juice concentrate*
> *zest of 1 lemon*
> *juice of 1 lemon*
> *2 cloves garlic, crushed*
> *1/2 tsp ground cumin*
> *2 tbsp fresh coriander, finely chopped*
> *125ml (1/2 cup) gold tequila or mescal*

Marinade the wings overnight in the well-blended margarita mixture: tequila, orange juice concentrate, zest, juice, garlic, cumin, coriander, and a little salt and pepper to taste. To cook, drain the wings and place under a medium-high grill for about 25 minutes, until cooked all the way through, turning regularly.

TEQUILA MARINADE

This marinade is perfect for barbecues – slap it on your meat at least a couple of hours before cooking, and preferably the night before, and leave in the fridge. Makes enough to coat 1 1/2 to 2 kilos (3-4 lbs) of beef steaks or similar.

> *2 tbsp sesame oil*
> *2 tbsp Dijon mustard*
> *1 tbsp balsamic vinegar*
> *2 cloves garlic, crushed*
> *1 tsp salt*
> *1 tsp black pepper*
> *3 tbsp tequila*

Mix all the ingredients together in a bowl. Add the meat and coat well, then seal the lot in a container with a lid or a tightly-wrapped bag.

WATERCRESS SALAD WITH TEQUILA TANGERINE DRESSING

This is a simple little salad given an extra tang by the introduction of the world's finest agave-based spirit.

> *For the dressing:*
> *65ml (1/4 cup) fresh tangerine or orange juice*
> *65ml (1/4 cup) vegetable oil*
> *2 tbsp fresh lime juice*
> *2 tsp honey*
> *1 clove garlic, crushed*
> *salt and pepper to taste*
> *2 tbsp tequila, preferably gold*
>
> *For the salad:*
> *3 large bunches watercress, with the stems removed*
> *2 tangerines or 1 small orange, peeled and divided into segments*
> *75g (3 oz) radishes, thinly sliced*
> *55g (2 oz) spring onions, finely chopped*

Mix all the dressing ingredients in a bowl and allow to sit for a while to blend. Then, in a large salad bowl, toss the watercress and half the dressing together, then add the other ingredients. Serve with the other half of the dressing on the side.

FROZEN MARGARITA PIE

All the ingredients of a fine margarita go into this pie, which doesn't require any baking. Leave plenty of time for it to freeze, however.

>*75g (3 oz) pretzel sticks, finely crushed*
>*150g (6 oz) sugar*
>*125g (4 oz) butter, melted*
>*zest of 1 lime*
>*125ml (1/2 cup) fresh lime juice*
>*1 tin (400g / 14 oz) sweetened condensed milk*
>*280g (10 oz) whipped cream*
>*2 drops green food coloring*
>*12 mini pretzels or thin pretzel sticks, for topping*
>*4 lime slices, very thin and halved, for topping*
>*2 tbsp gold tequila*
>*2 tbsp triple sec*

Mix the crushed pretzels, sugar and butter in a medium bowl. Press the mixture firmly into a buttered, 22cm (9 inch) pie dish and chill in the fridge for an hour. Meanwhile, combine the lime zest, juice, condensed milk, tequila and triple sec in a bowl, and fold in 1/3 of the whipped cream, and the colouring. Pour this mixture into the pie crust and freeze for at least four hours. To serve, top with the rest of the whipped cream and scatter with pretzels and lime slices.

OTHER SPIRITS & LIQUEURS

"I feel sorry for people who don't drink.
When they wake up in the morning,
that's as good as they're going to feel all day."
Frank Sinatra

GRAVLAX

Gravlax was originally made in the middle ages by Nordic fishermen who would pack the salmon in salt and lightly ferment it by burying it on a sandy beach above the high-water mark. You can replicate such genius with a little patience and your choice of spirit. Aquavit, brandy, gin, vodka (including flavoured ones) and Pernod all work well.

> 1 (1.2-1.8kg / 3-4lb) salmon
> 3 tbsp salt
> 2 tbsp sugar
> 1 tsp freshly ground black pepper
> 1 large handful fresh dill, roughly chopped
> 1 tbsp spirit of choice

Fillet the salmon but leave the scales on. Place both halves, scales down, on a plate. Sprinkle with salt, sugar, pepper and dill, then splash on the spirits. Place the two halves together, scales out and tails together, and wrap tightly in clingfilm. Put another plate on top, weight it down with something weighing at least half a kg (1 lb), and stick it in the fridge.

For 2-3 days, unwrap the clingfilm every twelve hours or so and baste with the juices. When ready to eat, slice very thinly, at an angle, and serve with toast or crackers and lemon wedges.

BAKED MACKEREL WITH CALVADOS

One of Lord Bone's favourites this. "Drinking Calvados while cooking is optional," he says, but we suspect it's not exactly frowned on. Serves 2.

> 2 mackerel, cleaned and heads removed
> 30g (1 oz) butter
> 3 large spring onions, chopped
> grated rind of 1/2 lemon
> 50g (1 3/4 oz) white breadcrumbs
> 1 tbsp fresh parsley, chopped
> 1 medium Bramley apple, cored and finely chopped or
>   mashed
> oil
> 2 tbsp calvados

Pre-heat oven to 190C/375F/Gas Mark 5. Wash and dry the mackerel. Melt butter and gently fry the spring onions for about 2 minutes. Combine apple, spring onions, calvados, parsley and breadcrumbs in a large bowl, and season well with salt and pepper. Pack an equal quantity of the mixture into the belly of each fish. Brush the fish with oil and season with a little more salt and pepper. Place the fish in a foil lined baking tin and bake in the top half of the oven for 25 minutes.

PISCO COOKIES

These *alfajores* are a South American speciality, particularly popular in Argentina and Uruguay, but found throughout the continent, and often sold in 'white' and 'black' versions, coated in chocolate. This version doesn't include the chocolate – but feel free to add your own.

> 6 tbsp butter, softened
> 80ml (1/3 cup) cornflour
> 150g (5 1/2 oz) plain flour
> 1/4 tsp baking powder
> 1/8 tsp salt
> 175g (6 oz) sugar
> 2 large egg yolks
> 1/4 tsp vanilla
> 100g (4 oz) dulce de leche
> icing sugar
> 1 tbsp pisco (brandy will do in an emergency)

Preheat the oven to 180C/350F/Gas Mark 4 and butter a large baking sheet. Whisk together the cornflour, flour, baking powder and salt in a small bowl. Separately, beat the butter and sugar in a large bowl, then beat in the egg yolks, pisco and vanilla. Stir in the flour mixture until well mixed and if the dough is sticky add 1 or 2 tbsp more flour until soft. Roll out the dough to about 3mm (1/8 inch) thick and cut out cookies – a 4cm (1 1/2 inch) cookie cutter is perfect, and will make about 32 rounds.

Put these on the baking tray with some space between them and bake for 12-15 minutes, until firm and pale golden around the edges. Allow to cool, then stick the cookies together in pairs with about 1/2 tsp of dulche de leche each. Dust with the icing sugar to serve.

SEDUCTION ROLLS

This recipe is from a wonderful book by Isabel Allende, *Aphrodite: A Memoir of the Senses*, and is intended as foreplay to a more substantial meal... It uses Pisco, the national drink of both Allende's birthplace Peru and her native Chile.

> 100g (4 oz) cream cheese
> 2 tbsp butter
> 2 tbsp cream
> 1/2 tsp ground pimiento or paprika
> 1 tbsp lemon juice
> Salt and pepper to taste
> 4 thin slices ham or turkey
> 1 tbsp pisco

Combine the cheese, butter, cream, pimiento or paprika, lemon juice, pisco, lemon juice, salt, pepper and pisco in a bowl and mix well. Spread on the meat and roll into tubes. Cover with foil if you want to save them in the fridge until later. Serve sliced into inch-long logs.

DOUBLE CHOCOLATE GRAND MARNIER BROWNIES

Alexandre Marnier-Lapostolle liked cognac so much, he moved there and started blending it with Caribbean *Citrus bigaradia* oranges, considered quite the thing in 1880. The result was Grand Marnier.

> *55g (2 oz) dark chocolate*
> *55g (2 oz) milk chocolate*
> *2 eggs*
> *110g (4 oz) butter*
> *175g (6 oz) granulated sugar*
> *150g (5 oz) flour*
> *1/2 tsp baking powder*
> *1/4 tsp salt*
> *55g (2 oz) pecans, chopped*
> *1 tsp vanilla*
> *2 tbsp Grand Marnier*

> *For the frosting:*
> *55g (2 oz) milk chocolate*
> *2 tbsp cream*
> *2 tbsp butter*
> *130g (4 1/2 oz) confectioner's sugar*
> *1 tbsp Grand Marnier*

Make these at least 24 hours ahead of time. Preheat the oven to 180C/350F/Gas Mark 4. Melt the chocolate by placing a bowl in a pan of heated water, then add the sugar, eggs and butter. Mix the other dry ingredients, then add to the chocolate, stirring well. Finally, stir in the vanilla. Place in a greased 20cm (8 inch) square tin and bake for 25 minutes. As soon as they're out, brush them with the Grand Marnier and leave to cool.

For the frosting, melt chocolate and butter together. Stir in the cream and Grand Marnier, add the icing sugar, and spread on the cooling brownies, then leave for 24 hours.

SAMBUCA JAM

If you like Sambuca like I like Sambuca (which is a lot, by the way) and you want something with a little extra to spread on your toast, this is just the thing. Makes 5 half-pint jars.

> 1 kg (2 1/4 lb) fresh blueberries, crushed
> 1 tsp lemon zest
> 125ml (1/2 cup) water
> 350g (12 oz) sugar
> 1 box light fruit pectin
> 50 coffee beans
> 125ml (1/2 cup) white Sambuca

Mix a third of the sugar and the pectin together. In a large, heavy saucepan, stir together the blueberries, lemon zest, water and Sambuca. Cook over a high heat, stirring constantly, until the mixture is boiling hard. Stir in the remaining sugar, and bring back to the boil, stirring constantly. Boil for another minute, then remove from the heat.

Place 10 coffee beans in each jar, then immediately pour in the hot jam and seal tightly. Leave to cool for some time.

DAKOS ME OUZO

Dakos me Ouzo are a meze speciality from Crete, similar to bruschetta. This recipe uses the traditional feta cheese as it's usually easier to find, but if you can find the harder *myzithra* cheese, that works even better.

> *8 small slices of toast*
> *1 large ripe tomato, peeled and finely chopped*
> *65ml (1/4 cup) of olive oil*
> *1 tbsp oregano*
> *225g (8 oz) feta cheese, grated*
> *125ml (1/2 cup) ouzo*

Mix the tomato, olive oil, oregano and a dash of the ouzo in a bowl. Leave it to sit for a good half an hour to blend. Moisten the rusks under the cold tap (don't let them get soggy), sprinkle them with the remaining ouzo, spoon over the tomato mixture and top with the grated cheese. Drizzle with olive oil to serve.

SFAKIANOPITES

Sfakianopites are small cheese pies from the beautiful, mountainous region of Sfakia in south-west Crete – another ouzo-based meze.

> *600g (20 oz) plain flour*
> *2 tbsp olive oil*
> *salt*
> *1 cup of water*
> *500g (18 oz) myzithra or romana cheese*
> *2 tbsp ouzo*

In a large bowl, mix the flour, oil, salt, water and ouzo to make a soft dough. Roll it to a 1/2 cm (1/4 in) thick and user a small saucer (or 12cm (5 in) diameter cutter) to cut it out in circles. Roll the cheese into golf-ball size lumps and place in the centre of the circle of dough, placing another circle over the top and pinch the edges together. In a hot pan, fry the pies with little or no oil until browned on both sides. Serve hot, drizzled with honey.

CREVETTES AU PASTIS

"How do you know when a Frenchman has been round your house? The bins are empty, and the dog's pregnant." It was a Frenchman who told me that, and he did so after we'd consumed a large quantity of his family's home-made pastis. Nothing quite like it for firing the blood.

> *3 tbsp butter*
> *450g (1 lb) fresh shrimp, peeled*
> *1 fennel bulb, chopped*
> *250g (9 oz) double cream*
> *1 small red pepper, chopped*
> *3 tbsp pastis*

Heat a third of the butter over a high heat, and sauté the shrimp for 2-3 minutes, until just pink. Pour in the pastis and flambé, then remove the shrimp from the pan, leaving the juices. Add the fennel and cook for about ten minutes, until translucent. Add the cream and the pepper, and slowly bring to the boil, reducing the cream slightly, until it thickens enough to coat the back of a spoon. Return the shrimp and heat through, then serve.

Arak Cookies

Arak, which originated in the Eastern Mediterranean, lays claim to being the very first liqueur, created when aniseed berries were added to distilled palm wine as far back as 800 BC. The first historical mention of arak occurs 2,500 years ago, and it spread rapidly through the Middle East and North Africa. Ouzo may be substituted, but arak is the real thing.

> 450g (1 lb) butter, softened
> 125g (4 oz) icing sugar
> 4 egg yolks
> 750g (1 1/2 lb) plain flour
> 1/2 tsp baking powder
> 225g (8 oz) blanched almonds, finely ground
> 6 tbsp arak

Preheat the oven to 180C/350F/Gas Mark 4. Mix together the butter, sugar and egg yolks until creamy. Mix the arak in well, then sift in the flour and baking powder. Knead into a firm dough, then add the nuts and knead again. Press the dough into small cookie shapes about 5cm (2 in) across and bake in the oven for 20-25 minutes. Sprinkle with a little more icing sugar and allow to cool.

AMARETTO SPINACH SALAD

The legend of Amaretto goes that in 1525, a church in Saronno, the liqueur's home town, commissioned the artist Da Vinci and his student Bernardino Luini to paint their sanctuary. As the church was dedicated to the Virgin Mary, Luini needed to depict the Madonna, but was in need of a model. He found his inspiration in a young widowed innkeeper, who became his model and his lover. Out of gratitude and affection, the woman wished to give him a gift. Her simple means did not permit much, so she steeped apricot kernels in brandy and presented the resulting concoction to a touched Luini. The story is, in all likelihood, bollocks, but it's a nice story. And this is a nice salad.

> 900g (2 lbs) spinach, washed and shredded
> 450g (1 lb) olive, diced
> 125ml (1/2 cup) salad oil
> 2 cloves garlic, crushed
> 125ml (1/2 cup) red wine vinegar
> 125ml (1/2 cup) lemon juice
> 4 tsp Worcestershire sauce
> 1 tsp dry mustard
> 125g (4 oz) mushrooms, sliced
> 1 small red onion, sliced
> 125ml (1/2 cup) Amaretto

To make the dressing, place the bacon in a large pan and cook over a medium heat until crisp. Set the bacon aside add cook the garlic in the fat, adding the oil, vinegar, lemon juice, Worcestershire sauce, mustard,

Amaretto and a little salt and pepper. Simmer until blended then cool.

When ready to serve, place spinach, mushrooms, onion and the bacon in a large bowl and toss in the dressing.

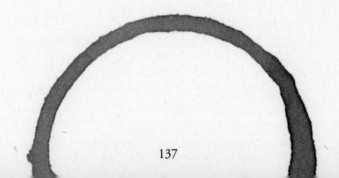

AMARETTO MOUSSE

This light, nutty little number makes 6 scrumptious servings, perfect for the tired palate.

> 1 pt whipping cream
> 1 tbsp gelatin powder
> 4 eggs
> 3 tbsp icing sugar
> dash vanilla extract, to taste
> dash almond extract, to taste
> 1 cup toasted almonds, chopped
> 125ml (1/2 cup) Amaretto

Whip the cream and stick it in the fridge until ready to use. Heat the Amaretto very gently in a pan – just enough to dissolve in the gelatin. In another pan, beat the eggs and sugar over a gentle heat, then remove and whisk until the mixture forms firm peaks. Fold the gelatin mixture into the eggs, then fold in the whipped cream. Add the vanilla and almond extracts to taste, and place in suitable glasses in the fridge for at least an hour. Garnish with the chopped almonds to serve.

AMARETTO SPUMONI

Spumoni is the original ice cream, originating from Naples and giving birth to the famous Neapolitan ice cream we know today. This simple version is courtesy of my friend Max. "Makes loads," he says – or "about 9."

> *9 egg yolks*
> *8 tbsp caster sugar*
> *300ml (10 oz) double cream (lightly whipped)*
> *amaretti biscuits to serve (one per serving)*
> *1 wine glass of Amaretto ("Fill it up")*

Whisk the egg yolks with the sugar until creamy. Slowly add the amaretto and continue whisking. When all the Amaretto is mixed in, fold in the whipped cream. Pour into glasses (flutes look great if you can fit them in) and freeze. To serve, crush an amaretti biscuit and sprinkle on top. "Eat. Eat another."

GINGER SYLLABUB

Advocaat (or *advokatt*) is a rich and creamy liqueur made from eggs, sugar and brandy, named for the lawyers of the Netherlands who first took it to their hearts and gullets. Its creamy consistency makes it a great base for plucky puddings like this syllabub.

> *2 heaped tbsp ginger marmalade*
> *250ml (1/2 pint) double cream*
> *1 or 2 large pieces of ginger, chopped*
> *4 tbsp Advocaat*

Blend the Advocaat and marmalade, in a machine if possible, but otherwise by whisking hard. Whip the cream and mix that in too. Decorate with the chopped ginger and chill to serve.

ADVOCAAT ICE CREAM

Or, to give it it's proper, Polish name, *Lody z Kremu Jajkowego*. This freezes pretty hard, so get it out the freezer a little while before you want to eat.

> 300ml (1 1/2 cups) double cream
> 300ml (1 1/2 cups) single cream
> 5 tbsp white sugar
> 175ml (3/4 cup) Advocaat

Beat the double cream until it forms soft peaks, then add the single cream and sugar, beating until it again retains its shape. Add the Advocaat and fold in very gently. Transfer to glasses or a plastic mould, splash a little more Advocaat on the top, and freeze.

Acknowledgements

There are too many people to thank in a work of this kind, but I must extend my deepest gratitude for their advice, support and drinking habits to my mother and father, who know who they are, to my grandmothers Eva and Nancy, to my publisher and mentor Emma Barnes, and to my dear friends Mrs Alex Bridle, Mr Howard Gordon-Martin, Mr Edward Arthur, Mr Max Halley, Mr Tord Johnsen, Mr George Walkley, Mr Tom Armitage, Mr Chris Heathcote, and, for giving and enduring so much, Mr Tom Masters.

INDEX

143